# GOBEKLI TEPE

## AN INTRODUCTION TO
## THE WORLD'S OLDEST TEMPLE

### (REVISED EDITION)

## AVI BACHENHEIMER

This is a pre-publishing edition.
It requires further interpretation,
complementary data and
corrections.

Library of Congress Cataloging in Publication Data
Data available

 BIRDWOOD

For Klaus Schmidt
(1953-2014)

## PREFACE

The current revised edition of Gobkli Tepe, an Introduction to the world's Oldest Temple is based on a pre-publishing edition of the book which was released in 2016. The original book was a collection of field reports I had prepared and edited in 2012 when I visited Gobekli Tepe as part of the archaeological efforts led by Klaus Schmidt.

The revised edition released now is divided to 5 chapters. The first chapter explores hunter gatherer communities of the Near East during the Last Glacial Maximum at around 26,000 BP to the advent of the Natufian culture. This had to be done for a basic reason that the people of Gobekli Tepe were descendants of the hunter gatherers of the region and chronologically they are placed in a period of time where transition from a hunting and gathering form of life to agriculture is evdient across the Near East. The second chapter on the other hand is focused on this transition and how climatic conditions of the age, and geographical properties of the region facilitated the emergence of sedentism and agrarian form of subsistence. This is the time period in which Gobekli Tepe was constructed, based on the best radiocarbon dating estimates. The third chapter narrows down the scope of analysis to Gobekli Tepe's location, topography and its environs. It explores some important structural aspects of the site, such as the enclosures and furthermore historical context of Gobekli Tepe's discovery. In chapter 4 I have investigated the significance of T-shaped pillars in the context of Gobekli Tepe's architectural features and those of the regional settlements concurrent to the construction of the sanctuaries. In the following chapter, complementary information is provided concerning the usage of the site, some of the more interesting finds and its placement in Near Eastern communal practices of the age.

Apart from the narrative based delivery of the first chapter, the remaining segments of the book have a clear archaological undertone. I have attempted to provide as much information by the captions of photographs, graphs and regional maps to complement the reader's possible lack of information concerning complicated areas explored. Deductions are based on archaeological and scientific methods and they do not diverge towards hypothetical speculative and imaginative falsehoods plaguing the current discourse with respect to the site.

Each parapgraph is assgined with a reference number. Citations and information sources for the data provided are respectively noted in chapter 6. The chapter furthermore contains additional readings that the audience might be interested to explore.

Avi Bachenheimer May 2018

# TABLE OF CONTENTS

# CHAPTER 5
## Complementary Features of the Site

# CHAPTER 6
## Bibliography, References, Notes and Further Readings

# 1

## CHAPTER ONE

### LIFE AND LAND USE IN THE
### LATE PALAEOLITHIC OF THE NEAR EAST

## Weathering the Last Ice Age

The cold had taken a toll on the human population across the entire planet. In Europe alone, the number of Homo sapiens across the higher latitudes had dwindled into the dismal figure of a few hundred. Freezing ice sheets had laid waste to the once thriving grasslands of Siberia. The Taurus mountains were covered by the glaciers extending throughout the central Anatolian Plateau, smothering the last remaining land bridge that connected continental plains of Europe and Asia to one another. For over half a dozen millennia, for six periods of a thousand years, the continued existence of human life across the planet had been at risk. From 25,000 to 19,000 years ago the gates of cold hell had been set wide open. The Last Glacial Maximum had begun, and what was at stake was the prospects of a human species on the verge of near extinction.

Just like the Neanderthals perished in the pages of history, humans were at the sight of a precipice moving fast towards them. Life in the Last Glacial Maximum had been a blitzkrieg of ongoing struggle. A routine labour of holding out against temperatures of up to 9 degrees lower than the current. The remaining pockets of human hunter-gatherers across the world had all retracted to a handful region of retreat known as refugia - enclaves of habitable space sprinkled in reduced numbers across the lower latitudes of contiguous Eurasian steppe zones. These were the only liveable stretches of land capable of hosting Homo sapiens of the northern hemisphere. Severe plant shortage and lack of food resources were incurable and to the hunter-gatherers of antiquity, the upsurge in cold had been a terrible setback, a disaster in the making with just a few survivors.

The last inter-glacial warm period had ended a few thousand years back, sometime close to 34,000 BP. Ever since, the world had witnessed a rapid and steady decline in temperature. Time had long passed since the days of humanity's mass exodus out of

Figure 1. During the Late Glacial period, tundras dominated the landscape near the ice sheets. With permanent frozen subsoil, tundras could have only hosted small shrubs and low growing trees.

Figure 2. The eruption of West Antarctic Mount Takahe coincided with the final phases of the Last Glacial Maximum. The eruption lasted for well over 200 years creating a conical volcano 780 kilometers wide with a summit range of 8 kilometers.

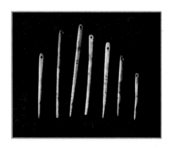

Figure 3. Evidence of sophisticated technological and cultural transitions of the Late Glacial period could be found in bone tools of intricate design and craftsmanship. Here, a set of 17,000 year old bone sewing needles of the Late Palaeolithic period are displayed from Courbet Cave in France, Europe.

Africa. The journey which had been taken by the Sapiens of the Middle Palaeolithic, 50 thousand years or so earlier. Those ones who saw first hand, the pleasant, warm and hospitable climatic conditions of the planet were of course all gone. The remaining species of fauna, capable of weathering the numbing cold were all littered in sparsely distributed horizons, effectively meager to sustain less than a million human lives scattered across the whole world. Scouring for food, roaming around the woods for shelter and water and hunting the wild species at hand, for long had been favoured as the modus operandi of a hunter-gatherer's life. In short, the mere pursuit of survival was analogous to practices such as scavenging and foraging for sustenance. A large extent of time spent by Homo sapiens on the planet and a good proportion of evolutionary optimisation had taken place in such an unpleasant set of conditions.

1.3

For over two hundred generation of Homo sapiens, grappling with the worst ordeal set forth by the nature - the Last Glacial Maximum - opulence had never been a thought entertainable. One chance, and they could have proven themselves capable of turning the tides, but for thousands of years, the tide never turned. The cold persisted. The world has always been a rough and rugged terrain. All the physical strengths and cognitive capacities in humanity's possession, had to be mustered to combat destructive forces of nature, and even then, the die hard climate of the day countervailed. With a large cache of powerful natural disasters, it strove against the Sapiens. Closer to the end of what we know today as the last ice age, and at about 21,000 years ago, entrenching cold draughts engulfed the entire planet, only coming to pass in a sudden upsurge of perforating solar irradiation in the course of the next one thousand years. By 19,000 BP simultaneous volcanic eruptions under the West Antarctic Ice Sheet immersed the planet in a thin layer of ash. It continued for over two hundred years. When eruptions ended, an outburst of global warming triggered the rise of sea levels. The end of the ice age had neared, with all its uncertainties.

1.4

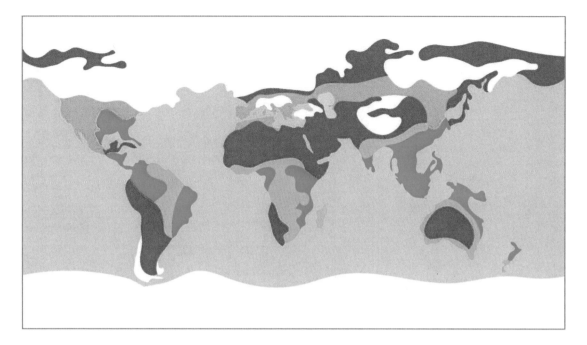

The ascendence of Homo sapiens has been as much attributed to their genetic excellence, as to the impact of nature's ceaseless pressure employed to put them down, once for all. Catastrophes forged their will and stamina into solidity of survival. The nature had thrown every trick in the book of the creation at this crowd, but they had refused to capitulate. One could see their daring spirit of defiance reflected in their material culture, in their tightly woven strands of clothing, their impenetrable leather leggings, fur jackets and their worn-out grass shoes. Humans never gave in. They were built to outlive the frigid conditions. They were conditioned to outpace the rumbling of thunderstorms and to outmatch the ferocious passion of the giants, the likes of mammoth megafauna, sabre-toothed tigers and mastodons. Their meticulously hand-made stone tools of intricate design were forged with the sole aim of bursting and tearing through the wild-life flesh in the most effective way. The ones that emerged out of the ice ages, also made use of bone tools, antlers, wood and ivory. Their microlith blades and bladelets were the first in the history of life on the planet - specialised tool types with specific purposes. Hides were

Figure 4. Map of the world during the Last Glacial Maximum. Ice sheets are shown in white and open seas in light blue. Red areas display the extent of deserts and light green demonstrates the presence of shrublands accompanied by dark green that stands for open woodlands. Tundras and sparse steppes are represented in dark yellow. Across the Near East, the majority of what is known as the Anatolian peninsula had been covered with thick layers of ice. The Caucasus and the highlands of the Zagros were also dominated by freezing climatic conditions. The rest of the landscape was a barren ground incapable of hosting shrublands, grasslands or dense forests. By the end of the last ice age at around 18,000 BP this all would change and the Near East would be covered with a panoply of botanical forms.

1.5

Figure 5. Chauvet cave in southern France contains some of the most fascinating forms of creative and innovative expressions of cognitive capacity of ice age hunter-gatherers. Illustrations on the walls of the cave are dated back to about 32,000 years ago when humans settled in southern peripheries of European glaciers. The evolution of Homo species to the point where they were capable of manifesting their personal feelings and collective perception of the world in such an incredibly meaningful ways was indicative of a great leap forward, a revolution of the kind that enabled abstract thinking and logical reasoning. Subjects of these artistic works are often wild hoards of animals that are now have been long extinct. Their depictions can help us in determining what the environment across southern Europe looked like during the ice ages.

worked, harpoons were made, eyed needles were forged and fishing became a central aspect of their lifestyle. Their complex technologies of creating hafted weapons, their representation of symbolic behaviour, figurines and art were all testaments to their zest, evidence of their zeal for excellence.

The survivors of the ice ages, went on to outlive any other member of the genus Homo on the planet - to rule over the world all by themselves, for the first time in 6 million years. The one and only Homo sapiens. With the Neanderthals long gone, the Homo erectus was too consumed by the forces of nature. Homo floresiensis followed suit and there last came the Denisovans. They too were devoured by the harsh climatic conditions of the ice ages.

1.6

Human hunter-gatherers of the Late Palaeolithic period were not only resilient, they were also cunning, versatile and flexible.

18

They traversed vast swaths of land in quest for preys, in pursuit of other predators, in search for suitable crops and trees producing desirable seeds. All this had been done with the knowledge of concurrent seasonal changes in vegetation cover, annual fluctuations in temperature and changing patterns of precipitation across landscape. These foragers and hunter-gatherers were the most alert and the sharpest of all the living beings. They grew hardened in bands. They drew from the power of cooperative and coherent action. Their developed modes of communication marked a new era of cultural growth and having shouldered the grave burden of humanity's fate, they took on themselves to impart on their offspring every means of survival - manifest in technologies that were passed down to their descendants in knapping styles, tracking skills, cordage weaving and canoe making.

Ancestral traditions were vouchsafed to the young in languages unique in nature, preserving tales, myths and memories of generations, and celebrating Homo sapiens impressive endurance against the bitter climate of the time, the rise in temperature and the upsurge in sea levels that followed the last ice age. They came out of the Last Glacial Maximum, the most dynamic they had ever been in the history of the primates, the most dominant they had ever been in their rivalry with the wild and the untamed. They had grasped a better understanding of the unknown. Rich in material culture, their descendants practicing long traditions of tool-making developed in the Levant, fanned out across the expanding liveable plains of Asia and the opening terrain against the receding glaciers of Europe. Lithic industries such as Ahmarian and Emiran, dominant technologies of tool-making by the end of the last inter-glacial warmth phase - 35,000 years ago - were carried along accompanied by local developments of Gravettian to the north and Antelian across the southern latitudes of Eurasia. Technical knowledge associated with these cultures were the likely sources of abrupt and rapid takeover of the planet in all directions, notably the crossing of the Bering

Figure 6. Skull cast of a sabre-toothed cat distinguished by its long curved blade-like canine teeth and powerful clenching jaws. The species were some of the most distinctive predatory animals of the Late Glacial period. Scavenging on the corpus of prey brought in by large carnivores including the likes of a sabre-toothed cat had remained a consistent componenet of human subsistence strategy since the rise of Homo erectus 2 million years ago. By the arrival of Holocene at 10,000 BP and the end of the Last Glacial Maximum, all members of the cat-like megafauna mammal went extinct.

Figure 7. Carved from mammoth ivory, Venus of Brassempouy was discovered in a cave in southwestern France in late 19th century. The female figurine belongs to the Gravettian culture of the Last Glacial Maximum in Europe, a local development of a chiefly Near Eastern tradition of tool-making from the Levant.

1.7

1.8

Figure 8. By the end of the Last Glacial Maximum, tundras were replaced by steppe grasslands. These biomes were capable of hosting a wide range of species which were dependent on their vegetation cover.

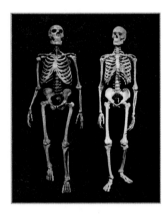

Figure 9. Morphological features of a Homo sapiens sapiens (right) in comparison with that of a Homo neanderthalensis (left). Neanderthals had a larger cranial capacity and a broader rib cage. Their bone structure was dense and more compact than that of a human. They were stocky and short and cognitively were capable of showing some properties of a sapiens-like species. A limited percentage of human genome (1.5 percent) is influenced by that of Neanderthals, indicative of their interbreeding during the last ice age. No evidence has emerged yet that is capable of showcasing hostilities between the two species. The last Neanderthal probably lived in southern Spain at around 20,000 BP. By that time this Homo species had gone virtually extinct.

Strait towards Americas. The crucial lessons of the ice ages were thus preserved across the entire colonised planet. To live and to prosper, the wild had to be rendered meek and in that path, no subjection was deemed adequate. The world had to surrender in full submission.

**The Post-Glacial Near East**

Eighteen thousand years ago, the world entered a new phase of post glacial climatic period. Ice sheets capping the continental landmasses of Asia, Europe and America began to subside as a result of naturogenic causes. So too, with global warming trend on the rise, vegetation cover across the planet went under sudden transformation. Tundras gave way to the arrival of temperate grasslands and steppes. Europe, central Africa, east and south-east Asia, Siberia, north and central Americas had all forgone a dramatic change in humidity and temperature, and closed forests and woodlands were appearing across the terrain all-over. Humans were now trailing the heels of a well-suited climatic optimum, beginning by 17,500 BP with cycles high in temperature increasing across seasons, giving birth to a wide range of naturally occuring plants and grazing animals. Blessing for the man, the rise in sea levels over 120 meters above the glacial average, had served as an obstacle to our modern attempt to gain knowledge of the human past. The lower riverine valleys and costal plains all over the world were inundated by the upsurge, concealing sites that could have contributed the most to our of understanding of the lives of hunter-gatherers of the last ice age. After all, a page had turned and a new chapter in the life of Homo sapiens had begun.

1.9

For generations, successors to the Homo sapiens of the Last Glacial Maximum inhabiting the western lowlands of the Zagros and the rocky terrains of the Levant, were in command of the Near Eastern landscape. By the end of the ice ages, these mobile hunter-gatherers heralded a reorganisation of nomadic practices across the region, unprecedented in history. The most prominent of them all were called the Kebaran and the Zarzian traditions, respectively dominant in the coastal regions of the Mediterranean Sea and over the hilly flanks of the Zagros mountains. For over 6,000 years, technological developments - often shared amongst the two cultures and sometimes distinctively dissimilar - were the driving forces of revolutionary experiences across the land. Itinerant people of the two traditions followed a particular seasonal habit of migration identical. One that although had originated in the last ice age, it had never been exclusively practiced as an independent mode of life. Over the lower ridges of a contiguous set of mountains encircling the central terrain of the Near East, the Kebaran and the Zarzian took refuge throughout the summertide and warm seasonal cycles of the year in rock shelters and natural hillside caves. When winter would arrive, they were resolved to move towards the lowland plains

1.10

Figure 10. The Wright Valley in Antarctica as it looks today, resembles what Siberia must have looked like during the last ice age. With high mountains surrounding the landscape and low humidity, Siberia during the Last Glacial Maximum was a free dry land, the likes of which could have been observed across a wide expanse of Europe and Asia. Dry deserts of low humidity were common throughout the northern hemisphere, in specific across the Near East and the surrounding valleys of central Asia.

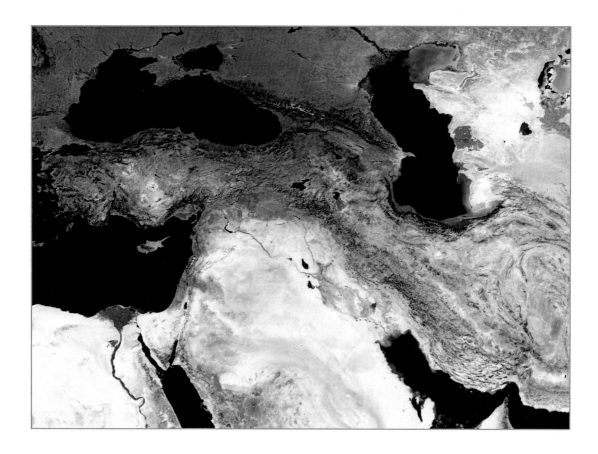

Figure 11. Satellite imagery of the Near East surrounded by the five seas of antiquity and flooded with running rivers of Tigris and Euphrates. The Near East as a term is ascribed to the overall swathe of land that encompasses the western end of the Asian continental plate. It excludes regional territories to the north of the African Middle East. To the south, the terrain is barricaded by the Arabian desert and across the north, it enjoys a lush green climatic condition. The earliest settlements in the world were founded across lowlands of the southern strip of this green stretch of land, that continued from the mouth of the Persian Gulf, traversing a sickle-shaped distance towards the Levantine Corridor.

adjacent to the mountains, near the meadows and inland bodies of water. Their nomadic movement followed a rigorously regular and consistent pattern of life. Conditioned by a preferences for stability and predictability, they constructed the first and the most basic temporary structures in history, kidney shaped huts with rubble foundation of various sizes which were covered by tree branches and brushwood. Ohalo near the Sea of Galilee is one of the type-sites of this period in the Levant. Following their recognisably unique habit of migration, the inhabitants traversed around a set of base camps with foraging ranges of up to 20 kilometers in radius. Along the hem of the mountains and treading through the land, their journeys were not taken unaided. They were accompanied by their shadow companions - the man's best friend.

Surviving through the throes of the last ice age by the side of their human counterparts, were members of a distinct wolf-like species of canine commonly known as dogs. The post-glacial population of the Kebaran were the first of the humans in the Near East to live alongside their domesticated beasts, taking advantage of their companionship in their daily routine and in essential tasks such as guarding their encampments, hunting, snaring and taking down games. The Kebaran and the Zarzian had in addition adopted a particular strategy of hunting for sustenance that was remarkably ingenious and dynamic. They used advanced technological innovations of the time, eccentric to the commonly known traditions of the preceding Late Glacial cultures. Evidence for the use of bows and arrows appear first in the Kebaran phase of the Near Eastern archaeology. Arrow shaft straighteners have been unearthed near the lip of the Euphrates throughout the northern Levant in a litany of sites associated with Late Palaeolithic of the region. Confident in the wealth of their up-scaled toolkit, the prospect of chasing a variety of games across a panoply of environmental habitats had been made exceedingly open at this point. Intrinsic and mental modification, commitment and communal approach towards problem solving and application of logical reasoning, reinforced and amplified through the unfavourable course of the Late Glacial period, would now come into the assistance of the humans in forethought, planning and execution of tasks. This was translated quickly into a remarkably mobile apparatus of nomadic life, embraced consciously by the Near Eastern post-glacial hunter-gatherers - the Kebaran, the Zarzian and the late-comers of the Late Palaeolithic of the region; Natufians - all alike. Where technological, social and cultural advances enabled a substantive rise in total amount of daily intake and diversity of the sustenance, these hunter-gatherers intensified their exploitation of the natural resources available in sight. For a dozen generations to follow, peculiar populations of western Asian genetic foment, come into presence across a wide array of geographical regions in southern Europe, central Asia, south

1.11

Figure 12. An east-west view of an Ohalo kidney-shaped hut unearthed near the See of Galilee in modern day Israel. Seasonal residences of the kind were common during the Kebaran period of the Near East.

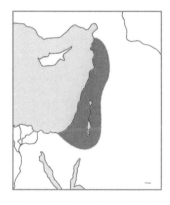

Figure 13. The Levantine corridor of the eastern Mediterranean shoreline is accredited to be the genesis of agricultural practices. Rubbing shoulders against the southwestern continuatioon of the Golden Triangle, the region served as a contributing locus to the Neolithisation of the Near East. Immediately after the end of the last ice age, this corridor was inhabited by the people of the Kebaran culture, a distinct tradition of tool-making with an identical semi-sedentism mode of living.

Figure 14. Hilly flanks of the Zagros mountains in Kurdistan, where the Zarzian tradition flourished through the course of post-glacial period. The Zagros ranges contains some of the highest peaks throughout the region, with overflowing rivers, snow capped mountains and lowlands suitable for a variety of vegetation covers.

Figure 15. Tigris and Euphrates in the core agricultural zone of Mesopotamia - the land between the rivers - are the most prominent waterways of the region. The two originate in the highlands of the Taurus Mountains in Turkey 1,750 kilometers to the mouth of the Persian Gulf. Their near confluence in southern Iraq contributes to the creation of the Central Iraqi Marshland. Over the Anatolian peninsula, the Halys river runs across the plain in a crescent-shaped pattern for over 1,355 kilometers, brushing against the farthest extensions of the Euphrates and producing a sequence of watercourses that stretch out from the Persian Gulf to the Black Sea.

Asia and the Caucasus, indicative of a significant population growth of Near Eastern origin.

The Near East - a landscape to describe the western Asian geographical plain, stretches out from the eastern coast of the Mediterranean Sea all the way to the central plateaus of Iranian interior. It extends for over 1,900 kilometers in expanse. Paradoxical to the place-name derived from a European perspective of the universe, the Near *East* in essence is the *centre-most* point of convergence across the Eurasian landscape. Tucked away in form of an over-reaching land bridge that further ties the two continents of Europe and Asia to the African plate, the region appears synonymous to a three-way intersection positioned in the crux of the world and resembling an inter-continental nexus.

1.12

The Near Eastern centrality is not a property of sheer geographical significance. Its historical and pre-historical prominence lies in the way in which the overall terrain harboured an inflow of cultural and technological breakthroughs of various continental origins, all coalescing in a focal point of intermixture. The body of land itself is a confined ground, capable of harvesting the thrust of incoming innovations in a plethora of insulated and secluded local enclaves. It is surrounded by the rocky mountains of the Taurus fault zone to the north and the Zagros fold belt to the east and is overflown with fresh-water rivers of Tigris and Euphrates, streams of Halys and Zab and tributaries of Karkheh and Karoun near the lip of the Persian Gulf. Merely a thousand years after the end of the Last Glacial Maximum, the terrain was already unrivalled in richness of its local fauna, abundance of rain, ampleness of its plant life and plenitude of solar irradiation absorbed. This was the humans vantage point of contact with the wild. Their most suitable battle scene with the forces of nature, where they proved to be an effective constant in the multi-variable function of the events unfolding across the world.

1.13

## The Garden of Eden

The hard-won struggle was fought in the heart of the ancient Near East. From millennia, the five seas of antiquity, risen to the shorelines of this plain had provided its coastal sanctuaries with a litany of marine life, ranging from shellfish to sea-birds, crabs, turtles and mammals. The Mediterranean Sea had encircled the vast plain over the west, locking arms with the coastal plains of the Black Sea to the north and the appendages of the Red Sea towards south. The largest in-land lake of the planet, known as the Caspian Sea rested across the northern flanks of the Iranian Plateau which in turn was skirted to the south by the Persian Gulf - with its farthest reaches advancing against the central lowlands of the Mesopotamian basin and subsequently the Arabian Peninsula. From the Near Eastern centremost point of convergence, the open seas of the world could be accessible in nearly every direction.

1.14

Figure 16. Natural grasslands of wild wheat and barley near the Hasan Dagi double-volcano in central Turkey. The mountain is the second highest peak of the Taurus ranges and was a source of obsidian and valuable rocks in antiquity. The richly induced volcanic surroundings of the mountain in Palaeolithic period attracted hunters and gatherers of the region to the vicinity of the mount collecting cereals, legumes and wild species of wheat.

Figure 17. Shanidar cave in Iraqi Kurdistan was home to hundreds of generations of humans and Neanderthals alike during Palaeolithic period. The cave inkeeps remains of some of the oldest species of Homo sapiens sapiens unearthed out of Africa. It also contains evidence of various Neanderthal remains that shed light on not only the radius of Neanderthal expansion across the world but also on Neanderthals practices and modes of cognitive expression. Shanidar cave also displays evidence of the Zarzian tradition, contemporaneous to the Levantine Kebaran of the Late Palaeolithic.

Proximity to the known high seas of the world was not the sole characteristic of the region in sight. Volcanic zones of the Near Eastern sierra, well over the shoulders of the Zagros and the Armenian highlands, had put in disposal of the hunter gatherers of the Late Palaeolithic the finest of obsidian cores, suitable for knapping incredibly sharp razor-edged stone-tools unrivalled in practice. There, for the taking, was the cutting edge technology of the age, presented to the artisans of the post-glacial Near East at large. Projectiles made out of these glass-like stones were the likes of modern day's most effective weaponry. Annual migration of animals with certain seasonal patterns, guaranteed a deluge of matching prey to the excellence of these huntsmen's calibre. Where the wild traversed the landscape - near the lowlands of the Zagros and the Taurus, a hunter's dream would come true, a prime piece of paradise was put on display.

1.15

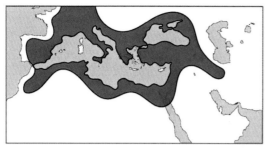

Map A. Showing approximate location of the Mousterian culture in southern Europe, northern Africa and the Near East (150,000-45,000 BP)

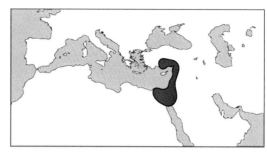

Map B. Showing the extent of the Ahmarian culture across the Levant and Sinai peninsula (48,000-42,000 BP)

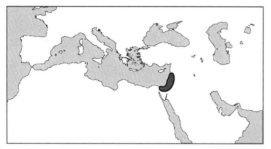

Map C. Approximate location of the Emiran tradition across the Levant (48,000-39,000 BP)

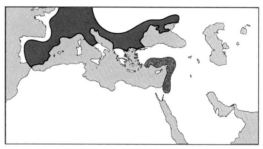

Map D. Approximate location of the Gravettian tradition in southern Europe (32,000-18,000 BP) and the Antelian across the eastern coast of the Mediterranean Sea (34,000-12,000 BP)

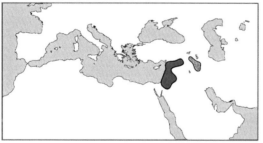

Map E. Showing approximate locations of the Kebaran (18,000-13,000 BP) to the west and the Zarzian (20,000-10,000 BP) to the east of the Near East

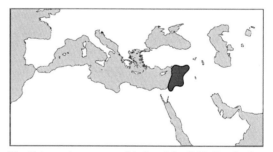

Map F. Approximate extent of the Late Palaeolithic Natufian in the Near East (15,000-11,000 BP)

Figure 18. Late Palaeolithic traditions of tool-making across the Near East, Mediterranean coastline and southern Europe. The Late Palaeolithic refers to the period throughout which significant material remains associated with Homo sapiens activities are unearthed out of Africa. Beginning at around 50,000 BCE, the Late Palaeolithic age often known as Epipalaeolithic period extends as recent in time to 12,000 BCE when the earliest evidence for Neolithic markers appear across the world. Mousterian archaeological industry, a Middle Palaeolithic tradition originating at around 150,000 BCE is deemed to be the main linkage to the Late Palaeolithic culture.s Appearing across a vast horizon of the known world, it was practiced at around every major coastline of the Mediterranean Sea by 45,000 BCE. It is followed subsequently by Ahmarian, a Levantine industry of tool-making that was further proliferated in Europe as Aurignacian and across the Levant as Emiran. The two eventually evolve into Antelian and Gravettian cultures, respectively across the Levant and in southern Europe. Near the end of the Last Glacial Maximum, the Antelian culture is replaced by two distinctive but similar industries of the Kebaran and the Zarzian in opposite terminations of the sickle-shaped mountain ranges of the Near East. Natufian, the last culture of the Late Palaeolithic period and the foremost of all in its significance was an off-shoot of the Kebaran industry. It originated in the northern Levant and was subsequently practiced across the entire Near East.

Figure 19. For thousands of years, obsidian rocks had been a valuable source of tool-making for hunter gatherers of the Near East. Some of the projectile points carved of the volcanic rock core are shown here. The penetrating power of the lithic makes it one of the most effective hunting tools man had ever made in prehistoric times.

Figure 20. Natufian shell necklace from Ma'aret a-Nahal near the Sea of Galilee. Ornamental grave goods such as pendants and necklaces are typical to the Natufian type-sites of the period. They are often accompanied with stone tools and artefacts indicative of long distance trade and intra-regional communications. Burial practices are often complex, where human remains are interred in pitholes accompanied by remains of various animals, plants and grave goods. The Natufian toolkit is also rich in various forms of microliths, blades and bladelets, mortars and pestles, bone tools, harpoons and arrowheads. Natufian settlements were semi-subterranean with stone foundation and were inter-connected to one another in a constellation of camps often two dozens kilometers distant.

In Wadi el-Natuf overlooking the plains adjacent to the Mediterranean shorelines of the Levant, several communes of the Kebaran culture, flourished into the espousal of sedentism and food procurement by 14,000 BP. Three millennia after the receding ice-sheet glaciers of the LGM had waned, vegetation cover across the region was dominated by grass, legumes and herbs. Evidence of seed collection and food processing in early Zarzian culture of the northern Zagros at Palegawra Cave and the Kebaran Ohalo have been encountered in past, dating to the earliest phases of the world on the heels of a global warming, but the emergence of full sedentism alongside selective and intensified collection of wild cereals, nuts and legumes were some of the innovative markers of the upcoming Natufian culture. In other words, hunter gatherers of the Natufian culture were purposefully selective with what they foraged and they were scrupulous with what they hunted in the stead of being mere observants of available sources of sustenance at hand. In Zarzian for instance, Asiatic wild ass and wild sheep had remained for an exceptionally long period of time the main categories of prey, simply due to the fact that these species of fauna were the most prominent in number throughout the local habitat of the region. The fact is complemented by the Kebaran's dependence on a wide variety of species, turtles, birds, fish and medium sized herbivores as they settled alongside the coastal plains of open seas. Peculiar reliance of the Natufian subsistence on the other hand, on hunting and butchering gazelle, deer and aurochs is a property of sort uncommon to the preceding ages of the post-glacial world, as it demonstrates a form of preference in selection among the choices of wild present in the nature, a biased approach complemented by curious forethought and planning and most importantly collective hunting. Taken to another point, Natufian mode of year-long occupation as opposed to the seasonal settlements of the Kebaran and the Zarzian is prognostic of a profound transformation in the history of humankind's relation with the nature. Natufian culture is at the apex of the Late Palaeolithic

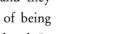

1.16

| Middle Palaeolithic period of the Near East | **46,000 BP** | Late Palaeolithic period of the Near East | **15,000 BP** | Terminal Phase of the Late Palaeolithic period |

| **12,000 BP** | PPNA of the Near East | **10,000 BP** | PPNB of the Near East | **9,000 BP** | PPNC of the Near East and the Pottery Neolithic |

traditions of the Near East, with its full-fledging characteristics of lifestyle and technology strengthening the hands of an upcoming Neolithic mode of life and agriculture - undoubtedly the most prominent of all transformations in human past. Gobekli Tepe resides in the final chapter of this cultural and economic transition. There the burgeoning sprouts of a Neolithic Revolution were laid.

# 2

## CHAPTER TWO

### AN ANALYSIS:
### THE LATE PALAEOLITHIC TO
### NEOLITHIC TRANSITION

## The Late Palaeolithic Transition

The question is what elementary factors contributed to the emergence of an agrarian lifestyle in the Near East? We have previously expounded on how accentuation of environmental constrains during the Late Glacial period and shortages of natural resources had compelled the human population of the planet to counter adverse external conditions of the time through seeking new, alternative and innovative practices. The Late Glacial changes in life-ways were chiefly behavioural in nature, leading to the evolution of mental faculties that were unprecedented in human history - properties that come into life across material evidence, following the last ice age, such as preference in selection of habitat, broadening of social interaction systems and a profound reliance on supplementary technological innovations. As an external variable, fluctuations in temperature combined with the internal operation of human agency in management of its surroundings were the two main contributors to the behavioural and technological transitions of the Late Palaeolithic period, without which the survival of mankind would have been rendered undoubtedly impossible.

Final phases of the Late Palaeolithic, following the last ice age, the coldest of the past 100,000 years, witnessed a surprisingly sharp and extremely rapid rise in temperature by 18,000 BP. Warming climatic circumstances beginning at around this time, facilitated growth of dense forests, woodlands and shrublands in Eastern Mediterranean region, southern Turkey and northern Iran. Across these domains, the amount of precipitation received in low-lying plains adjacent to the mountain ranges experienced a two-fold rise. Biomes rich in naturally occuring flora and fauna were essentially far more accessible to the Near Eastern populations of the periphery in comparison to the hunter-gatherers of the barren central core. Favourable conditions in supportive areas, instigated a transformation in human perception of its environment which was conversely reflected in

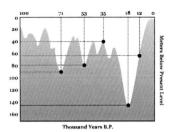

Figure 21. Fluctuations in sea level through the course of the last 100,000 years. Rapid rise in temperature at around 18,000 BP had an immediate impact on climatic conditions of the world. The Last Glacial Maximum was the coldest of all frigid periods and what followed was the sharpest rise in temperature and sea levels.

Figure 22. Remains of a rounded Natufian storage pit at Nahal Ein Gev II in the Jordan Valley. The settlement dates to 14,500-11,500 BP. Indications of full sedentism and storage optimisation across the site predate the Neolithic tradition of farming and animal husbandry. Nahal Ein Gev II demonstrates qualities of a transitional type-site across which all characteristics of a community in transformation of its Palaeolithic life-ways to a Neolithic one are evident. Intensive occupation of the settlement, expressions of art in forms of perforated stone and shell beads, bone tools, pestles and ground stones, high investment in architecture and storage facilities are all telling of a flourishing Late Palaeolithic culture on the cusp of the Neolithic Revolution.

a cognitive leap. Semi-sedentism of the Kebaran and the Zarzian, immediately following the rise in temperature are indicative of a reinforced management approach, where humans trusted the cyclical favourable climate of the time as a durable and a reliable external element, utterly in contrast to the harsh, frigid and unpredictable conditions of the ice ages. What appears to have contributed to the emergence of full sedentism by the Late Natufian period is an attempt made by the hunter gatherers of the periphery to harness the forces of nature in pursuit of manufacturing and creating conditions for a lifestyle reliable and stable, nonetheless more complex. Practices such as intensive harvesting of wild crops, food procurement and storage optimisation were subsequently developed in the Late Natufian period to amplify sustainable properties of sedentism, ancillary to the adoption of a low-risk preference in subsistence.

2.2

Scientific consensus in the last few decades has witnessed a clear divergence from theories type-casting the Levantine corridor as the impeccable cradle of stimuli leading to the emergence of agriculture, to a broader outlook that designates a network of regional communities scattered across the entire Near Eastern domain, culpable for the Neolithic Revolution. The newly surfaced picture, free from the notable biases of the past, has contributed in a remarkable way to the wealth of theories describing the origins of agriculture, animal husbandry and sedentism in the region. Inter-twined elements as they seem, properties that expedited the adoption of sedentism as an static and secure mode of living preceded generic aspects of farming and domestication of animals. Full-fledging agricultural societies appear only in the late 11th and early 10th millennia BP, unlike the earliest year-long huts and houses of the Natufian period which had been already in customary usage through the course of the Terminal Late Palaeolithic period, two millennia before the arrival of auxiliary Neolithic markers. Now we will discuss geographical and also environmental contributors to the adoption of an agrarian form of subsistence in the Near East.

2.3

## The Golden Triangle

Archaeological theories developed in the course of the last few decades describe multiple localities of the Near Eastern Late Palaeolithic, all contemporaneous to one another as collective contributors to the emergence of ingenious and ground-breaking package of Neolithic markers, the most notable of which were agriculture and domestication of animals. In the context of the overall archaeological horizon of the Near East, evidence on three Late Palaeolithic zones engaged in transition to neolithisation are distinguishable - the Levantine corridor, the hilly flanks of the Zagros and the parallel ranges of the Taurus mountains. Challenging a traditional hypothesis that takes a single nexus of settlements in one certain locality as the lead, current theories in contrast denote a range of regional developments responsible, with an initial unsystematic appearance of markers in a collection of towns to the fore and a subsequent intensification of those practices in a horizon better known as the Golden Triangle.

The Golden Triangle characterises a theoretical domain across which developing practices of neolithisation - in the context of our analysis, domestication of animals and crops - converge in a fusion core, where transition of ideas and populations from peripheral sites strengthen the hands of an agrarian subsistence against the traditional hunting and gathering way of living. Each one of the abundant and plentiful communities of the Golden Triangle is on part, an affiliated constituent of one regional Neolithic development amongst the three major Neolithisation horizons of the Near East. Therefore, the impact of Zagros cluster is relatively more profound on the southeastern communities of the Golden Triangle, where the influence of the Levantine practices are observed in the southwestern settlements of the cultural zone and the Anatolian ones over the northern contingent. Communities located in the integral core of the Golden Triangle are therefore culturally the richest and the most

2.4

2.5

Figure 23. A bone sickle of the Late Kebaran, early Natufian period of Ramat HaNadiv in Israel. Bladelets were hafted into the shaft in a continuous series creating a sharp-edged cutting tool which was used for harvesting wild crops and cereals adjacent to the settlement.

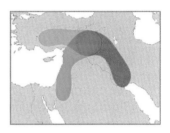

Figure 24. Map of the primary neolithisation zones across the Near East. Blue represents the expanse of the Levantine core. Green stands for the Taurus contingent and the red demonstrates communities of the Zagros ranges. The three coalesce in a theoretical domain often described as the Golden Triangle which is the point of convergence for the noted Neolithic traditions. The Golden Triangle in addition, is the sole geographical region of the Near East that contained wild forms of the founder crops (einkorn, wheat and barley) and the four main wild species of fauna (goat, sheep, cattle and pig). Technologies associated with the Neolithic Revolution were either local to the communities of the region or were transitioned through and from its adjacent settlements - which were part of the primary zones.

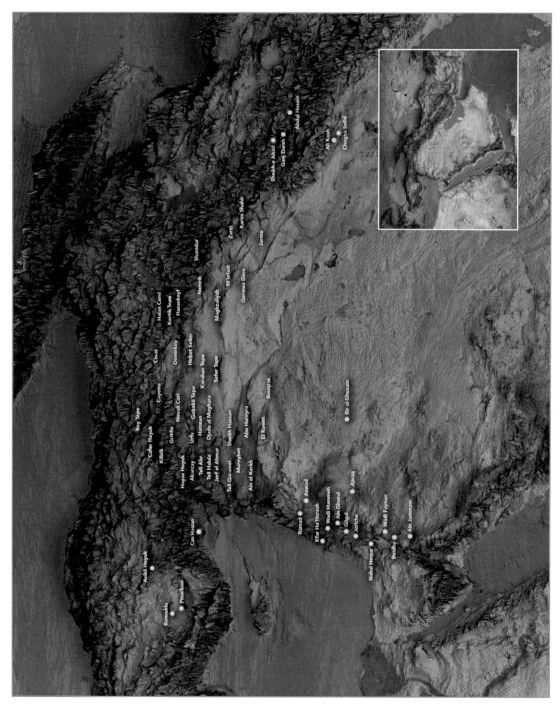

Figure 25. The Late Palaeolithic and Pre-pottery Neolithic settlements of the Near East. communities shown in red belong the core Neolithisation domain of the Golden Triangle whilst those shown in yellow fall out of the theoretical range. Those settlements in the interior of the Golden Triangle show incredible similarities not in the case of one or two Neolithic markers but with respect to a whole range of architectural, technologic and symbolic determinants of the Neolithic life.

36

elaborate of all settlements of the region. These in turn are so analogous in properties and characteristics of their physical remains to one another, that it appears the network of settlements were in clear coordination of experiential undertakings across time, through which they served as the locus of Neolithic lifestyle for the entire Eurasian landmass, wherefrom successful practices would fan out in all directions as a consequence.

In a reciprocal mode of collaborative coordination, a constellation of peripheral Near Eastern settlements received technological breakthroughs of the Golden Triangle in response to their own contributions to the practices of the central core. Case in point, as wheat and barley appear first in archaeological records of southern Turkey followed by the communities of the Golden Triangle, simultaneously people at the distant type-site of Ganj-Dareh in the Zagros mountains were experimenting with the earliest practices of taming wild goat - incidentally in the absence of any evidence for agricultural practices. As the local breakthrough of the Zagros origin will be transmitted to the core settlements of the Golden Triangle in the course of the following millennium, Ganj-Dareh itself receives in return technological frameworks for the domestication of wheat and barley through primarily Jarmo and Qermez Dereh and then Nemrik, with an origination source of Hallan Cemi in the heart of the Golden Triangle.

With that premise of significance accounted for, we are ought to contemplate on geographical and general climatic conditions of the region as a whole which are shared amongst the settlements of all neolithisation spheres - for the simple reason that these all were culpable each on their own part for initiation of various markers of the Neolithic period. The attempt to investigate common geographical characteristics in the continuum of the three major Neolithisation spheres of the Near East, brings us naturally to the consideration of the positioning of the

Figure 26. Earliest stratigraphic layers of Ganj-Dareh in the Zagros demonstrate the first evidence for domestication of goat, as they show simultaneously the absence of any agricultural markers. As people of Ganj-Dareh disseminate tradition of taming the wild goat across the region, they receive in return, agricultural practices of the Golden Triangle through the agency of their proximal settlements.

Figure 27. Architectural features of a Late Natufian hearth at Shubayqa, 14,600 - 12,000 BP - in Jordan (top) in comparison to that of a later Pre-Pottery Neolithic hearth constructed at Hallan Cemi 12,050-11,150 BP (bottom). The evidence indicates an evident transition of hearth-making technologies and traditions from the neolithisation zone of the Levant to the core of the Golden Triangle in 12th millennium BP.

| Site | Country | Period | Dating (cal BC) | Dating (cal BP) | 14C-age BP | Zone - Locality |
|---|---|---|---|---|---|---|
| Shanidar Zawi Chemi | Iraq | Middle Palaeolithic - Late Palaeolithic - PPN | 12,800 - 9,800 | 14,750 -11,750 | 12,455 - 10,115 ± 92 | Zagros - Iraqi Kurdistan |
| Abu Hureyra | Syria | Late Palaeolithic - PPN | 11,150 - 10,450 | 13,100 - 12,400 | 11,200 - 10,450 ± 102 | Taurus - Syrian Jezirah |
| Tell Qaramel | Syria | Pre-pottery Neolithic | 10,750 - 8,800 | 12,700 - 10,750 | 10,710 - 9,480 ± 40 | Taurus - Aleppo Plain |
| Karim Shahir | Iraq | Late Palaeolithic - PPN | 10,650 - 7,900 | 12,600 - 9,850 | 10,595 - 8,815 ± 69 | Zagros - Iraqi Kurdistan |
| Mureybet | Syria | Late Palaeolithic (Natufian) - PPN | 10,300 - 7,950 | 12,250 - 9,900 | 10,340 - 8,820 ± 147 | Taurus - Syrian Jezirah |
| Hallan Cemi | Turkey | Pre-pottery Neolithic | 10,100 - 9,200 | 12,050 - 11,150 | 10,270 - 9,690 ± 37 | Taurus - North of Sinjar |
| Qermez Dereh | Iraq | Late Palaeolithic - PPN | 10,100 - 8,850 | 12,050 - 10,800 | 10,270 - 9,490 ± 76 | Zagros - Iraqi Kurdistan |
| Gobekli Tepe | Turkey | Pre-pottery Neolithic | 9,750 - 8,660 | 11,750 - 10,610 | 10,105 - 9,375 ± 183 | Taurus - Harran Plain |
| Nemrik | Iraq | PPN - Pottery Neolithic | 9,700 - 8,200 | 11,850 - 10,150 | 10,170 - 8,975 ± 126 | Zagros - Iraqi Kurdistan |
| Kortik Tepe | Turkey | Pre-pottery Neolithic | 9,700 - 9,300 | 11,650 - 11,250 | 10,085 - 9,855 ± 14 | Taurus - North of Sinjar |
| Hasankeyf Hoyuk | Turkey | Pre-pottery Neolithic | 9,600 - 9,100 | 11,550 - 11,050 | 10,035 - 9,670 ± 118 | Taurus - North of Sinjar |
| Tell Abr | Syria | Pre-pottery Neolithic | 9,500 - 9,200 | 11,450 - 11,150 | 9,980 - 9,690 ± 110 | Taurus - Syrian Jezirah |
| M'lefaat | Iraq | Pre-pottery Neolithic | 9,500 - 8,800 | 11,450 - 8,750 | 9,980 - 9,480 ± 33 | Zagros - Iraqi Kurdistan |
| Jerf el Ahmar | Syria | Pre-pottery Neolithic | 9,450 - 8,550 | 11,400 - 10,500 | 9,965 - 9,295 ± 83 | Taurus - Syrian Jezirah |
| Demirkoy | Turkey | Pre-pottery Neolithic | 9,440 - 9,280 | 11,390 - 11,230 | 9,960 - 9,815 ± 12 | Taurus - North of Sinjar |
| Jarmo | Iraq | PPN - Pottery Neolithic | 9,100 - 6,950 | 11,050 - 8,900 | 9,670 - 8,015 ± 89 | Zagros - Iraqi Kurdistan |
| Dja'de | Syria | Pre-pottery Neolithic | 8,700 - 8,270 | 10,650 - 10,220 | 9,420 - 9,040 ± 42 | Taurus - Syrian Jezirah |
| Cayonu | Turkey | PPN - Pottery Neolithic | 8,650 - 6,750 | 10,600 - 8,700 | 9,365 - 7,895 ± 56 | Taurus - North of Jezirah |
| Nevali Cori | Turkey | Pre-pottery Neolithic | 8,600 - 7,950 | 10,550 - 9,900 | 9,330 - 8,820 ± 31 | Taurus - North of Jezirah |
| El Kerkh | Syria | PPNB - Pottery Neolithic | 8,540 - 8,320 | 10,490 - 10,270 | 9,285 - 9,125 ± 23 | Levant - Orontes Basin |
| Cafer Hoyuk | Turkey | PPN - Pottery Neolithic | 8,350 - 7,550 | 10,300 - 9,500 | 9,140 - 8,470 ± 48 | Taurus - Central |
| Gritille | Turkey | PPN - Pottery Neolithic | 8,000 - 6,800 | 9,950 - 8,750 | 8,835 - 7,910 ± 140 | Taurus - North of Jezirah |
| Akarcay | Turkey | PPNB - Pottery Neolithic | 7,900 - 6,100 | 9,850 - 8,050 | 8,815 - 7,225 ± 54 | Taurus - North of Jezirah |
| Halula | Syria | PPNB - Pottery Neolithic | 7,820 - 6,400 | 9,770 - 8,350 | 8,760 - 7,510 ± 25 | Taurus - Syrian Jezirah |
| Bouqras | Syria | PPNB - Pottery Neolithic | 7,500 - 6,300 | 9,450 - 8,250 | 8,400 - 7,405 ± 48 | Syrian Euphrates |
| Hayaz Hoyuk | Turkey | PPNB - Pottery Neolithic | 7,480 - 7,200 | 9,430 - 9,150 | 8,390 - 8,190 ± 32 | Taurus - North of Jezirah |
| El Kowm | Syria | PPNB - Pottery Neolithic | 7,100 - 6,350 | 9,050 - 8,300 | 8,105 - 7,485 ± 59 | Syrian Euphrates |
| Magzaliyah | Iraq | PPNB - Pottery Neolithic | 7,050 - 6,250 | 9,000 - 8,200 | 8,065 - 7,365 ± 54 | Zagros - Iraqi Kurdistan |
| Shimshara | Iraq | PPNB - Pottery Neolithic | 7,050 - 6,050 | 9,000 - 8,000 | 8,065 - 7,195 ± 20 | Zagros - Iraqi Kurdistan |

Figure 28. Late Palaeolithic, PPN and early Pottery Neolithic settlements of the Golden Triangle are listed out with their adjacent regional zones, calibrated age and the archaeological period to which they belong. Distinct sites of the regional neolithisation spheres are not included in the table. Note the placement of Gobekli Tepe as it represents a leap towards the Pre-Pottery Neolithic lifestyle alongside Nemrik, Kortik Tepe, Abr, M'lefaat and Jerf el Ahmar. Hallan Cemi Tepesi of the Taurus cluster predates Gobekli Tepe and is one of the most prominent settlements of the Golden Triangle before the construction of temple complexes across the region. On the other hand, the impact of the Levantine neolithisation sphere is evident in Abu Hureyra, Qaramel, Mureybet, Jerf, Kerkh, Bouqras and El Kowm.

mountains fringing the landscape at large, for their immense impact as external elements on subsistence strategies of the population is evident. To the east of the central frame of the Near East, the Iranian Plateau is positioned in sight which is effectively enclosed against its western division by the Zagros mountains. The range consists of a series of ridges that are shaped in parallel lines of extension, stretching out from northwest towards the central south, beginning from the southern Caucasus in a downward train towards the Strait of Hormuz in the heart of the Persian Gulf. Upon the Zagros chain, the Caucasus mountains, relatively short in expanse could be observed that are nonetheless of immense importance to the broader picture of the Near Eastern topography. The high mountains in essence, shaped in a form of a rampart function as a preventing barrier, obstructing passage from and through to the southern Siberian steppe zones of Eurasia. In that respect, concomitant to the natural barriers of the Caspian Sea and the

Figure 29. The Caucasus mountains to the northeast of the Near Eastern landscape effectively close off the region to the higher latitudes of the northern hemisphere, particularly the steppe zones of southern Russia and Siberia. Through the course of the Last Glacial Maximum, crossing the chain of mountains would have been almost impossible for the hunter-gatherers of antiquity as the peaks were covered with ice sheets and glaciers all year long. During the Late Palaeolithic period conversely, higher precipitation rate in winter time had made the surrounding plains of the mountains unliveable, whilst during the summer, its running rivers attracted bands of mobile humans to the region.

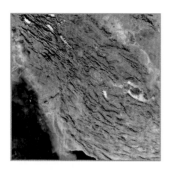

Figure 30. Satellite imagery of the parallel ridges across Zagros mountains near the lip of the Persian Gulf. Abritrary positioning of the lateral chains renders the Zagros domain impenetrable.

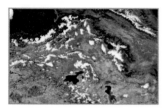

Figure 31. Satellite imagery of the Armenian highlands - a well scattered series of peaks to the east of the Anatolian plateau, that is positioned beneath the Caucasus and is located adjacent to the ridges of the Zagros.

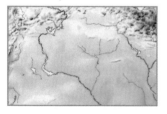

Figure 32. The Syrian Jezirah is a geographical plain to the south of the Taurus mountains that falls between the two main branches of Tigris and Euphrates. To the east, it is bounded by Khabur and the Sinjar mountain and through to the west it reaches the plains of Aleppo. Towards north, the Syrian Jezirah contains the Harran plain and the Balikh Dihliz where sedimentary depositions facilitates growth of diverse vegetation covers.

Black Sea to the opposite sides of its extension, the chain isolates the northern fraction of the Near Eastern landscape effectively altogether. The two ranges of the Zagros and the Caucasus reach a well scattered contingent of mountains to the east of the Anatolian Plateau that is chiefly known as the Armenian highlands. The Anatolian Plateau separated from the Arabian plate by the Titlis Suture is host to the Taurus mountains across its southern bank with its farthest extensions in the east, often known as the Anti-Taurus chain, reaching the base of the Armenian highlands. Unlike the Zagros mountains with sharp hilly flanks of high altitude, the high peaks of the Taurus mountains have a much lower elevation, which enables them to accomodate large open grasslands on both southern and northern parallels of the fault. This forms the central portion of sickle-shaped curvature of the Near Eastern mountains, positioned right above the tributaries of Tigris and Euphrates. Known as the Syrian Jezirah, the V shaped region is of immense archaeological value, as it is a major habitat rich in potential sources of sustenance, native birds and diverse forms of plants and animal life. To the southern convex of this pocket, overlooking the large swath of the Harran Plain towards the Upper Mesopotamian basin, major communities of the Golden Triangle - including Gobekli Tepe - in antiquity had flourished in abundant numbers. Towards the western extension of the mountains and on the hem of the Mediterranean Sea, a divergent continuum of the Taurus ranges are sprinkled opposite to the Mediterranean shoreline as they near the mountains of Lebanon. The chain is comprised of a cluster of low ridges and elongates downwards through to the Levant and the Golan Heights. It continues on its path further south to enwrap the plains of modern day Israel and Palestine to the west of its extremities. This is the final sharp spike of the sickle-shaped chain of the Near Eastern mountains. With rapid changes in elevation, it contains diverse concentration of biomes and is vastly rich in subsistence elements of Mediterranean fauna, shellfish and seafood. Across the Near East, the presence of diverse mountain

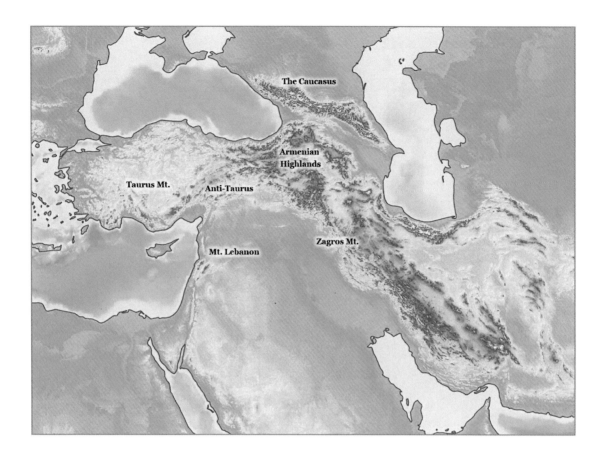

shapes and geological elements provide a landscape over which changes in altitude are converted into biodiversity of all forms, often present in both opposite verges of a ridge. If local, this heterogeneity would have guaranteed a variety of plants and animal forms throughout a district, but in the context of a closely knitted and interconnected mountain ranges of all configurations, stretching across the entire Near East, it appears to be strikingly exceptional and is hardly rivalled anywhere else in the world.

Today, physical features and geographical characteristics of the Near East at large, are very much alike to the conditions of the Late Palaeolithic period. Physical forms of elements such as valleys, hills, mountains and plateaus have logically remained for the most part unchanged in the last one hundred thousand years.

Figure 33. Topographic map of the Near East. Note the sickle-shaped configuration of the mountains as they begin from the mid-most section of the Persian Gulf, curving towards the Black Sea before falling southwards as they near the shorlines of the Mediterranean. Near the inward curve of these mountains, the most notable communities of the Late Palaeolithic and the Neolithic period had flourished in antiquity. Across these landscapes, favourable rates of precipitation, solar irradiation, suitable temperature and healthy soil provided a range of biomes across which adoption of sedentism appeared convincingly to be a reliable and secure choice.

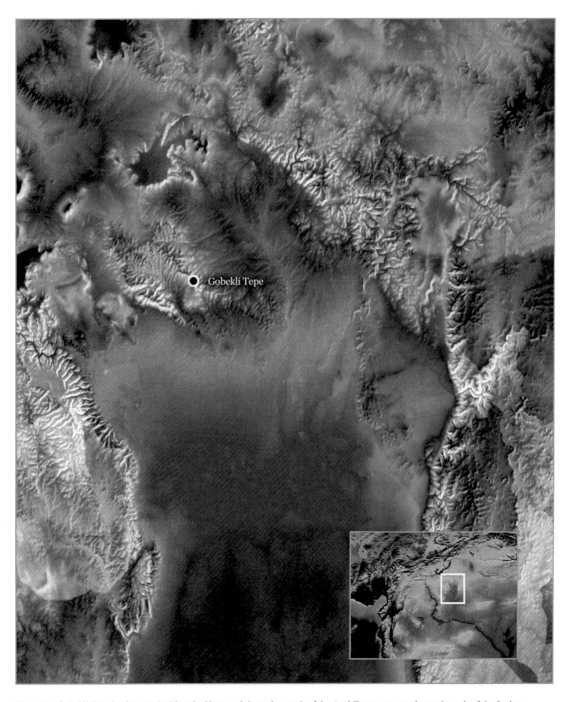

Figure 34. Gobekli Tepe in situ, overlooking the Harran plain to the south of the Anti-Taurus mountains and north of the Syrian Jezirah. Note the positioning of the site atop the intruding hills to the landscape. The hill captures a panoramic view of the lowlands adjacent to the ridge and provides visual access to the migration of wild species crossing the Balikh Dihliz in the Harran plain. The entire matrix of geographical features to the vicinity of the site resembles a concealed mousetrap, laid out to devour incoming herds of wild cattle, boar, gazelle and predators chasing them from the south.

The impact of human activities on these properties of the landscape are generally considered to be negligible as historically people of the Near East have always remained centred around particular domains and their interaction with the landforms constitutes a form of management throughout time rather than sheer alteration of the physical properties of the domain to a considerable degree. Nonetheless, a critical change in geographical configuration of the region requires further examination and its subsequent impact on the emergence of Neolithic practices is ought to be studied. This large-scale physical change is not yielded by humans of antiquity but in reality, it relies on the universal climatic transition of the world following the Late Glacial period. The issue at hand, relates to the bare volume of the surrounding open waters in the region, in particular the Persian Gulf and the Mediterranean Sea and the fluctuation of their surface levels in the last thirty thousand years - for the purpose of our study. At the end of the Last Glacial Maximum, rapid rise in sea levels across the globe accelerated the advancement of the Persian Gulf's shoreline inland, further through to the northwest - and mainly into the heart of what is known to be the Mesopotamian basin. 18,000 years ago, the lip of the Persian Gulf stood as far back as the Hormuz Strait. Following a regimen of universal rise in sea levels due to the melting of the ice sheets and glaciers, the sheer volume of the open waters carried in to the region increased exponentially for the next 13,000 years, reaching to its highest point by 5,000 BP. By this point, the coastline had advanced for an astonishing stretch of 1,100 kilometers from its initial stage, towards the central interior of the Near East, edging against the perimeters of Mesopotamian marshlands of Hur al-Huwayzah and Hur al-Hammar. Following the apex of 5,000 BP, the shoreline withdraws somewhat to its current position, slightly rearwards of its maximum expanse. Fluctuations of the Mediterranean sea level, follows a synonymous pattern. During the LGM, the eastern shoreline of the Sea was laid out 12 kilometers abaft, behind the modern day coastline, exposing an enormous expanse

2.8

Figure 35. A continuous line of ridges alongside the eastern coast of the Mediterranean Sea create a chain of high hills and low mountains that are represented chiefly by Mount Lebanon. The chain reaches the Golan Heights to the northeast of modern-day Israel and further advances towards southe till it reaches the Negev desert. The formation of these physical features of the landscape facilitated emergence of distinct Levantine cultures in the course of the Palaeolithic and Neolithic periods.

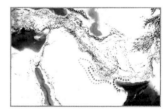

Figure 36. Map of the Near Eastern landforms during the Last Glacial Maximum. The expanse of open waters at around 18,000 BP is shown by the red broken line. The yellow line represents the farthest expansion of the Gulf into the interior of the Near East at about 5,000 years ago - carried for roughly 1,100 kilometers in to the interior of the region. The broken green line stands for the current coastline of the Persian Gulf.

Figure 37. The currently submerged Neolithic village of Atlit Yam in Israel is dated to 9,000 years ago when the coastline had not yet reached its modern day position. The underwater village contains massive stone circles similar to those of Gobekli Tepe in southern Turkey.

Figure 38. Southern Iraqi marshlands are the largest wetland ecosystem in western Asia. The rise and fall of the Persian Gulf sea level following the Last Glacial Maximum has contributed enormously to the formation of the low-lying grounds that are flooded in wet season and high tide. Changes in ecological and geographical features of the Near East during the Late Palaeolithic and Neolithic periods, not only did not hinder the emergence of an agrarian mode of life, but they facilitated the adoption of agriculture and domestication of the wild.

of continental ground, submerged today. Following a subsequent rise in temperature and therefore the upsurge in sea levels, taking place at the end of the Late Glacial period, the sea-line proceeded further inlands reaching its highest point around 5,000 years ago, when it plunged the terrain hosting the modern day city of Tel Aviv underwater. The impact of these fluctuations on archaeological records are not insignificant. The initial trend of post-glacial surge before reaching its maximum, resulted in the submergence of a 9,000 year old Neolithic village of Atlit Yam in modern-day Israel - a village that contains large stone circles not unlike those of its preceding type-site of Gobekli Tepe.

The rise in sea levels particularly during the terminal phase of the Late Palaeolithic period had a favourable impact on the emergence of flourishing settlements across the Near East. The phenomenon diversified sources of sustenance by providing further access to marine life and it had a downright positive influence on the amount of precipitation received throughout the region. Advancing sea levels carried in depositional sediments suitable for agriculture and contributed to the appearance of riverine landforms and marshes often remarkable for agrarian style of living. Taken the point to its end, modern geographical features of the Near East show unmistakable resemblances to the physical features of the land in the Late Palaeolithic period, that is in exception of the relative size of open waters surrounding the region. Sea levels have exponentially risen and slightly fallen over the last 18,000 years. This in turn is ought to be perceived as bearing an advantageous impact on the suitability of the region, as it underlines the merit of a hypothesis that describes the richness of the Near Eastern geography and its environmental characteristics as chief contributors to the transition from hunting and gathering to an agrarian form of life.

Threading the heels of a geographical examination of the

2.9

region's landforms and its surrounding waters, we can now focus on environmental and climatic characteristics of the Near East and the signficance of particular catalysts to the adoption of Neolithic practices. Palaeoclimatic condition of the region has been the subject of numerous archaeobotanical and palaeoenvironmental studies in past. Our arguments on the other hand, concerning the overall prevailing weather conditions of the Near East during the Late Palaeolithic period, relies on a distinct premise. That is, although changes in climatic conditions during the Late Palaeolithic and Neolithic of the Near East are undoubtedly irrefutable and the periodic recurrence of change in climate in the last 100,000 years is indisputable, the overall patterns of distribution, arrangement and abundance of certain climatic data across time have remained more or less uninterrupted. Let us elaborate on this by providing an example - given the intensity of precipitation across the region changing over time, nevertheless, patterns for distribution of rainfall across the Near East, for instance over its mountain tops, on the marshes, grasslands and elevated flanks of the mountains, have remained for all practical purposes unaffected. Synonymous to the pattern of precipitation, three other main environmental variants, contributing to the weather conditions imperative for the emergence of agriculture and domestication of animals in this part of the world, show compositional similarities. The three environmental qualities in addition to the pattern of precipitation previously noted are; soil salinity, average annual temperature and distribution of solar irradiation received across the region. Mapping out the arrangement of these four factors, reveals a shared continuous zone throughout which all the main environmental requisite elements facilitating the rise of agriculture and taming the wild are in favourable footing. The desired zone follows a sickle-shaped pattern analogous to the continuum of the mountain ranges through the region, a geographical phenomenon of significance that was discussed in previous chapters. The similarity further recalls distribution of the Late Palaeolithic and Neolithic settlements of the three main

2.10

Figure 39. Wall-paintings of Catalhoyuk, a Neolithic community of the central Anatolian Plateau depicting two vultures or cranes near a pair of wild horses or onagers. Close encounters of the kind with birds and wild species of animals is a commonplace theme of the PPN and Neolithic settlements of the Near East.

Figure 40. The arc-shaped formation of the Fertile Crescent - a continuum of favourable geographical and environmental habitats near the hills of the Near Eastern peripheral mountains, shown in red. The sickle-shaped region overlaps with the upper Mesopotamian extensions of Tigris and Euphrates, rendering the landscape incredibly diverse in the form of animals presented throughout. Various segments of the favourable horizon, fall into distinctive localities of neolithisation in the Near East, from the Zagros folds towards the east, Taurus mountains in north and the highlands near the eastern Mediterranean shoreline.

Figure 41. Green pasture grasses of this kind were attractive to the wild species of gazelle, sheep and aurochs. In the Near East of the Late Palaeolithic period, bands of hunter-gatherers were cognizant of a direct relationship between the favourable rich terrain and the diversity of animal life. They were also well-informed of the pattern of animal migration, knowing in advance where and when to expect the passage of a particular band of animals across terrain.

Figure 42. Wild lentil was one of the main categories of the founder crops, alongside emmer wheat, einkorn wheat, barley, pea and chikpea - all of which could be found in the arc-shaped favourable region of the Near East. Gobekli Tepe is situated in a region where all the categories of founder crops could be found out in the open. Reliance of hunter gatherers to sustainable wild sources of plant food was one of the driving forces of sedentism across the Near East.

spheres of neolithisation throughout the region - that is in turn not a sheer coincidence. Through the noted suitable zone, solar exposure is adequate, salinity of the soil is moderate, precipitation is abundant and average annual temperature is lower than the mean high temperature of the region.

Although correlation does not imply causation, our analysis demonstrates the existence of an appropriate geographical continuum that is supported by favourable environmental characteristics. The examination further highlights the fact that the Neolithic reliance on agriculture and taming wild variety of species, logically could have not and would have not taken place in any other localities of the Near East at large. In essence, if the convergence of appropriate geographical, environmental and ecological zones into a favourable continuum cannot be accounted directly for the genesis of the Neolithic revolution, the presence of such a theoretical landscape should be taken at least rationally as essential and prerequisite to the conditions leading the rise of agriculture and domestication of wild species. In the following chapter we will discuss how this favourable zone furthermore falls precisely within the terrain throughout which einkorn, wheat and barley - the founder crops - and lentil, pea and chickpea could have been found in the wild and untamed species of goat, sheep, cattle and pig were approachable in the habitat.

2.11

Neolithic founder crops, wheat, barley, einkorn and legumes are commonly described as cool-season pasture grasses. These founder crops are distributed in temperate climatic conditions across the planet, particularly in well-watered areas where abundance of sunlight provides a biome in which their conditions of growth are suitably met. Although known as cool-season grasses, the reliance of these primal crops on heat and solar radiation is critical in the course of their proliferation. An ideal landscape for the rapid increase of the founder crops in the wild is synonymous to the proposed continuum of suitable

2.12

Figure 43. Annual average temperature map of the Near East, Asia, Europe and northern Africa. Dark red represents the hottest and the warmest climatic conditions, followed by orange and yellow. Light green coloured areas are the regions with average mild annual temperature. In the Near East the green areas follow a curvature alongside the mountain ranges. Dark green and blue regions stand for cold climatic areas of the world where annual average temperature is well below the norm.

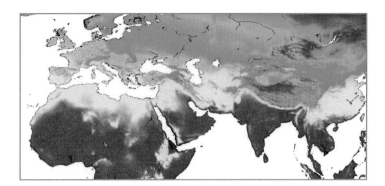

Figure 44. Map of solar irradiation across the Near East, Asia, Europe and northern Africa. Gradients of blue colour represent the highest amount of radiation received each year, while light green and fading yellow regions receive a relatively high to average amount of sun-light. In the Near East, the light green area and the fading yellow region receiving enough radiation to sustain growth of plant resources are found alongside the northern areas of the landscape in an arc-shaped form.

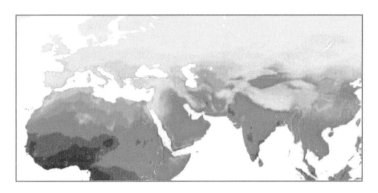

Figure 45. Map of the annual precipitation rate. Yellow stands for the lowest amount of precipitation received across the landscape (0-400 mm) while pink demonstrates an average of (800-1600 mm) suitable for plant growth and appearance of diverse biomes. Areas shown in dark blue recieve the maximum precipitation amount each year. In the Near East the favourable area follows an arc-shaped form alongside the mountains, in addition to the marginal regions alongside the Meaditerranean and the Black sea.

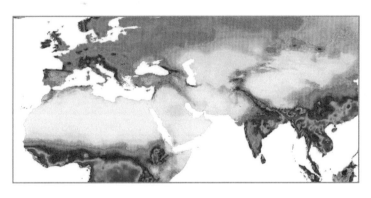

Figure 46. Map of soil salinity in the Near East, Asia, Europe and northern Africa. Green areas present the expanse of soil, favourable and healthy for agriculture. Pink areas demonstrate mildly favourable conditions while yellow and red stand for poor health and high salinity. Across the Near East a continuum of mildly favourable horizon is seen stretching along the mountain ranges of the region, accompanied by green healthy regions of northwestern Turkey and the Caucasus.

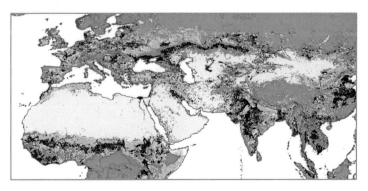

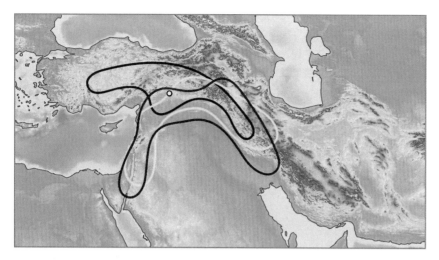

Figure 47. Distribution map of wild einkorn wheat, emmer wheat and barley across the Near East. Wild einkorn is indicated in dark blue, stretching to the interior of the Anatolian Plateau. Wild barley is shown in dark red and wild emmer in yellow. The crops are spread out along the arc-shaped Near Eastern favourable region. Gobekli Tepe is located in an area where all the three types were accessible in to the hunter gatherers.

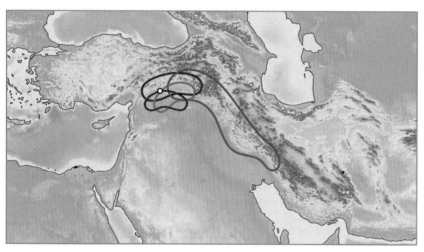

Figure 48. Distribution map of wild species of fauna throughout the Near East. Wild goat habitat is shown in blue, wild sheep in red, wild boar in green and auroch in grey. Gobekli Tepe is situated near the area of convergence of all the noted species of fauna. While goat and sheep are found in higher elevations and near the Zagros and Taurus ranges, auroch and boar are to be seen closer to the interior of the upper Mesopotamian basin.

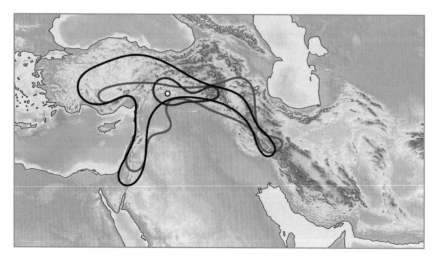

Figure 49. Distribution map of wild pea, wild lentil and wild chickpea across the Near East. Wild chickpea in red is only found to the southern areas of the anti-Taurus while wild pea in brown is to be found alongside the fertile crescent and towards the interior of the Anatolian Plateau. Distribution of wild lentil is shown in blue. Notice how Gobekli Tepe is situated right at the centre of a convergent area that is shared among all three.

climatic zone that was discussed in the course of geographical and environmental analyses of the region. This is a mildly temperate area that receives considerable amount of sunlight, with a precipitation rate well over the average and benefiting from a healthy soil with low concentration of dissolved saline elements - a region that favourably host a wide variety of naturally grown grasses, attractive to the wild animals of the late Palaeoithic period and logically the hunter-gatherers of antiquity in pursuit of those.

## Cultivating Crops

On careful management of available resources, the terminal Late Palaeolithic people of the ancient Near East were among the most economically advanced populations of their own time. Before the advent of agriculture, the Kebaran and the Zarzian hunter-gatherers of the region had adopted a semi-nomadic mobile mode of living, with seasonal migratory habits of movement that followed ecological changes through each of the four seasons of the year. In their close encounters with the habitat in which they lived, the Kebaran and the Zarzian inhabitants of the domain had a clear and sharp grasp of the geographical, climatic and ecological characteristics of the land. They had a distinctive intuition of what to look for and a profound perceptual capacity of where, when and how to look for it. They were well aware of the patterns of distribution of the wild crops across the region and understood the impact of where grazing grounds could be found, on arrangement of animal presence across the region. The Natufian culture that appeared immediately following the semi-sedentary cultures of the Late Palaeolithic was in essence the result of a rational leap in ancient inhabitants perception of the environment. If they knew where, when and how to look for their desired sources of sustenance, the logical question that followed was, is there a hypothetical landscape across which all their desired crops and wild animals supporting human dietary intake could be found in the vicinity

2.13

Figure 50. Natufian mortar and pestle made out of limestone. The prototype is of eastern Mediterranean origin. Natufian culture spread out alongside the coastal areas of the Levant and extended in the following millennia towards the southern Taurus region. Procurement of wild cereals using grinding stone tools was one of the main components of Natufian mode of life.

Figure 51. Interior decoration of house chambers at Catalhoyuk, one of the notable settlements of the Neolithic period in central Anatolian Plateau. James Mellaart, the original archaeologist engaged in excavations of Catalhoyuk considered these spaces to be temples. Today these rooms are known as communal structures, where people might have gathered to participate in feasts. Animal remains such as bull horns and bucraniums were used for decoration of strcutures throughout the settlement.

Figure 52. Gobekli Tepe in southern Turkey and near the modern day city of Urfa was constructed in mid-12th millennium BP. The site is comprised of several enclosures, each containing multiple anthropromorphic pillars. Gobekli Tepe was constructed at the time where Natufian people were in the course of a transition from a hunting and gathering mode of life towards an agrarian style of sedentism. The Terminal Late Palaeolithic structures of Gobekli Tepe are the oldest temple sanctuaries yet discovered across the entire world. In this photograph one of the unearthed sanctuaries of the Southwestern Depression, Enclosure C could be seen.

of, out in the open. Sedentism as a mode of living that relied far less on roaming about the land, only emerged in its heyday as chances of discovering such favourable horizons in the open appeared increasingly possible. The Natufians furthermore had amassed a toolkit of cognitive and perceptual systems, most suitable for the Near Eastern climate, that was technologically strengthened by a set of stone tools, better known as microliths, consisting of blades and bladelets geometric in design and directly chopped off the main core, facilitating the invention of sickles. In addition, as discussed in previous chapters the Natufians heralded the use of bow and arrow, obsidian daggers and most important of all, the heavy ground-stone tool.

Although sedentism and close proximity to the sources of cereals in the wild paved the way for a lasting and direct interaction with the environment, the sheer possibility of further contact does not necessarily translate into the adoption of practices such as impromptu cultivation of the land. The first kindlings of intentional practice of agriculture was set alight in the region, following extensive usage of what appears to be an accidental offshoot of an earlier invention, namely coarse-scraped grinding stone tools. Wild cereals known as the founder crops were harvested by the Natufians in the open during the course of rovering local target spaces for edible grains and wild animals. The first man or a woman who realised that a few grains wedded in to the cavities of the ground-stone were capable of germinating their own seedlings after a while, must have noted something to the likeness of Newton's explanation of universal gravity. Everyone had seen it, but no one had dared to spell it out. Others who had prowled back into the rounded storage camps in periodic inter-hunting hiatuses, in search of upcycling discarded tools or recovering long stored cereals, might have noticed the burgeoning sprouts coming out of the excess grains, but there was one individual who thought of putting them back in the ground for further reproduction. That one person, changed the course of human history, spearheading the rise of the Neolithic Revolution.

## Domestication of the Wild

The Neolithic Revolution in the Near East was by no means confined to the practice of agriculture. The Late Palaeolithic crusade of hunting the wild had already begun through the course of the last ice age with mental, technological and cultural ramifications, the most notable of which was near at-hand encounter with the prey. Confrontation of the hunter and the game must have triggered a cognitive exercise of reasoning that enabled humans to entertain the thought of keeping excess prey in reserve for additional supply or a time of need and trouble. From this point onwards, the challenge at hand had shifted from catching the largest and the most favourable prey to capturing the most manageable and the most docile. This was an imperative

2.14

2.15

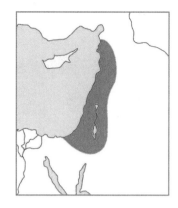

Figure 53. The Levantine corridor to the eastern coast of the Mediterranean Sea is accredited as the genesis of the Natufian culture. Rubbing shoulders against the southwestern continuation of the Golden Triangle, the region served as a contributing locus to the Neolithisation of the Near East in general and the development of agriculture and domestication of the wild in particular. Levantine corridor hosts a continuous range of archaeological sites beginning from the Middle Palaeolithic period all the way to the Neolithic era. The region is littered with rich cultural settlements and hunter gatherer camp-sites that contribute to our knowledge of prehistoric man.

Figure 54. Germinating seeds of wild wheat. Domestication of wheat and barley and einkorn had only been made possible when humans recognised that by planting their seeds in favourable conditions, they were able to reproduce them in higher numbers. The discovery resulted in an striking transformation in human lifestyle and heralded the advent of the Neolithic period.

Figure 55. Wall painting from the Neolithic settlement of Catalhoyuk, shows a man running in the course of a hunt while sporting a large leopard hide around the lower waist and abdomen. Implications of animal use across the PPN and Neolithic Near East are ubiquitous.

Figure 56. Bull horn decorations of Catalhoyuk (bottom) compared against wild goat horns, used for ornating communal structures at Sheikh-e Abad in the Zagros (top). Tepe Jani, Sheikh-e Abad and Abdul-Hussein, all in the Zagros neolithisation sphere predated the emergence of Catalhoyuk for over 2,000 years. It is speculated the communal practices of this sort, might have originated in the Zagros area at around 11th millennia BP.

condition to the process of taming and domesticating wild animals.

Implications of human interaction with the wild are evident in archaeological records of sites associated with the Zarzian, Kebaran and the Late Natufian Palaeolithic cultures of the region. Archaeological finds highlight everyday undertakings of inhabitants, centred around hunting, chasing and stalking the game in the open. This is more evident across the eastern domain of the Near East, near the hilly flanks of the Zagros where wild cereals were scant and gaining access to the ecological habitats containing them required long distance journeys to the lower plains adjacent to the chain of mountains. For this, the reliance of the Zarzians and the Late Palaeolithic population of the east on animal sources of sustenance was rather substantive. In Jarmo, across the Iraqi Kurdistan the earliest evidence of intentional selection of wild goat and sheep for domestication appears as early as 11,000 BP. In the entire upper Mesopotamian region befalling the landscape both inside and adjacent to the hypothetical sphere of the Golden Triangle, evidence for harvesting crops emerge gradually and continues on successively, hand in hand alongside with indications of taming the wild. In addition to onagers, goats, sheep and gazelles, the most dominant of the wild hunted across the east, the Taurus neolithisation sphere is immersed with faunal remains of a particular species of wild cattle, called aurochs. These were chased down the canyons and across the hills and were targeted in magnitudes unprecedented in the ice ages.

2.16

Venturing the landscape in pursuit of herbivores and the wild predators tracking the game, appeared to pose a much greater risk to the longevity of a human being than the sheer practice of cultivating harmless cereals. As emphasised before, this does not necessarily translate into a chronological timeframe supporting the emergence of agriculture before the appearance practices

associated with taming the wild. Some communities of the Near East such as Jarmo, Ali Kosh and Ganj Dareh, show forth a plethora of evidence that indicate domestication of the wild in those, preceded the emergence of agriculture. Others such as the majority of the Levantine settlements and those of the lower Taurus mountains, demonstrate an original farming way of life that is exponentially supplied with further intake of domesticated species. The note to be taken nevertheless is that the browbeating of the human and the wild was an elusive source of magnetism across the board, its attractions could be observed throughout the entire archaeological horizon of the Late Palaeolithic and Neolithic of the region in ancillary finds. The obsession with the beast of prey was a preoccupation of evolutionary magnitude, one that infatuated descendants of the Homo sapiens of the ice age with the allure of possessing the nature - the desire of the wild beast. Cultural finds for instance

2.17

Figure 57. Single room structures at Mureybet with hearths and storage spaces. Alongside Abu-Hureyra, D'jade, Kerkh, Sheikh Hassan and Tell Qaramel, Mureybet is one of the most important settlements of the PPN and Neolithic of the northern Levantine Corridor. With the advent of the Neolithic period, every single community of the region and the Near East at large demonstrates a transition towards agriculture and domestication of animals. The move towards Neolithic lifeways observed in Western Asia indicates the emergence of a cultural preference that dictated values of storage, food procurement and cultivation of crops in a universal manner. A paradigm shift in perception of the world.

Figure 58. Ibex or Persian Wild goat demonstrates extraordinary aptitude for climbing. Goats seem to have been first domesticated around 11,000 years ago in the Zagros mountains of Iran. Domestic goats were generally kept in herds that wandered around the hilly flanks of the ranges.

Figure 59. Cave art from the Indonesian island of Sulawesi are among the oldest ever examined. The finds discovered in rural areas of the island date back to well over 40,000 years ago. Hand prints are complemented with a relief of a goat which may indicate a mass migration out of Africa towards the southeast Asian islands of Sunda. The illustration demonstrates that interest taken by Homo sapiens towards animals and implications of their use and management had originated long before the advent of the Neolithic Revolution. Cave paintings this old and this complex have only been found in rock shelters of Epipalaeolithic Western Europe and later across the African Sahara, which was once a flourishing grassland filled with a variety of fauna.

are brimmed to the lip of the cup, with remains of bull horns decorating the interior architecture of housing. Objects which were extolled as symbolic totems of ferocity, life and death. Wall paintings show the course of ceremonies in which metaphysical forces were invoked to the abettance of tribes summoning good omens, crooning incantations while offering sacrifices. Leopard attires were sported as adornments to the frame of those celebrated huntsmen, who were praised as pinnacles of pride and honour of a settlement. Tusks of wild boar, teeth of foxes, claws of bears and talons of vultures were all used for purposes simply just beyond the needs and exigencies of a community's everyday life. The inhabitants of the region mastered and refined the art of animal manipulation to such an elevated level, that it is beyond the bounds of reason to assume that humanity would have been capable of undertaking the task of domesticating wild species in any other part of the world, but the Near East. Gobekli Tepe belonged to this transitory stage in human history where feasts and banquets were held in celebration of successful hunts and glorious game-chasing adventures.

## The Birthplace of the Neolithic Settlements

Throughout the transitory period of the Terminal Palaeolithic to the Neolithic of the Near East, communities of the Golden Triangle were in the forefront of humanity's cultural and economic breakthroughs. In these satellite communities, which now in conjunction with the settlements of the Levantine corridor and those of the Zagros ranges were spearheading socio-economic changes, Neolithic practices of harvesting crops and domesticating animals were refined and perfected. Situated north of the Syrian Jezirah, Cayonu witnessed an collective shared reliance on domesticated wild goat and cattle. Its diversified economy in addition, was sustained by an increasing dependence on cereals such as einkorn and emmer. In Hacilar across the western extension of the Taurus, wheat and barley were cultivated en mass. The first herds of wild boar were kept

and bred at Hallan Cemi. Nevali Cori was the scene for the emergence of a community entirely reliant on domesticated sheep. Abu-Hureyrah, Mureybet and Kerkh from the Levantine sphere, each at various stages brought the process of domestication of cereals further onwards. These economical transitions from hunting and gathering to an agrarian style of living - reflected in material remains - are discovered in increasing rate of domesticated plants and animals unearthed, in comparison to the remains of the wild taxa. Radical progressions of the kind noticed across every single site of the region, testify to the genesis of an over encompassing culture, a unified system of belief in which the essential expertise of engaging with domesticated animals, and cultivating the land were not just a case of simple preference, but they were a testimony to a community's worth and value. A cultural revolution in popular perceptions of prosperity and security was in the making.

Figure 60. Reconstruction of a Neolithic house from Catalhoyuk. The settlement had a population of well over 5,000 people and is well-known for its densely constructed houses that were accessible through the rooftop. Many of unearthed spaces at Catalhoyuk contain evidence of secondary animal usage, such as wall decoration of bull horns and objects such as pendants and figurines made of animals remains, bones and teeth. Catalhoyuk is one amongst a long list of Near Eastern Neolithic communities that demonstrate an exponential rise in reliance on domesticated source of food.

2.18

Figure 61. Auroch depiction at Catalhoyuk (bottom) compared against engraving of an auroch on a temple pillar at enclosure H of Gobekli Tepe (top). Similarities indicate the prominence of animal throughout not only the course of the PPN Near East (Gobekli Tepe) but also across the Neolithic period (Catalhoyuk) and the importance of wild cattle as a source of sustenance for domestic usage, feasting and ceremonial practices that was preserved through millennia.

Figure 62. Recovered animal bone spatula from Gobekli Tepe. The plaque is broken and with missing pieces. It has two T-shaped pillars imprinted on it with lines etched inside them. (L 5.3 cm, W 1.9 cm)

At the core of this final collective transition of socio-economic, technological and cultural magnitude, Gobekli Tepe nestled in dazzling glory as the earliest and the first temple-structure ever built in human history. This was not a settlement. Gobekli Tepe was the brain of the apparatus that sustained the mass movement's machine towards the Neolithic revolution. Here, the late Palaeolithic population of the region on the cusp of the Neolithic revolution, began to experiment in large-scale regional magnitude, not with agriculture or pottery, but with the craft of collective cultural thinking - the result of which appeared in intricate and elaborated design of temple-structures at Gobekli Tepe. The site was the cultural core of the movement - a movement that further reflects in intra-regional transition of artefacts, technologies and abstract ideas, and finally the advent of sophisticated domestic structure, pottery and burial practices. From the heart of the Golden Triangle, from the generations that saw and witnessed the construction of temples at Gobekli Tepe, people spread out in all directions, with ways of thinking and attitudes pre-conditioned to the exercise of symbolic and ceremonial traditions as prerequisites for agriculture and taming the wild. They carried their enlightening gospels and their unique perceptions of life to the continental Europe, central and east Asia and across the entire known world. Gazing at the sight of structures they had created in the Near East, they bore a belief in their heart, that they were capable of undertaking far more than anyone in past had ever entertained possible.

2.19

## Archaeogenetic Analysis

The study of ancient DNA in the last two decades has contributed to our understanding of the earliest physio-morphological and cultural developments associated with adoption of farming and taming the wild during the course of the Near Eastern Late Palaeolithic and PPN periods. Archaeogenetic analyses have been able to explain patterns of dispersal for three distinctive categories of inquiry. The first series of hypotheses attempt to describe genetic configuration of the early Neolithic founder crops. In that respect, archaeobotanists concerned with remains of plants cultivated and used by the early Near Eastern farmers, have been able to decode the genetic rate of growth and mutation of the target wild cereals. This paves the way for discovering the original point of initiation for each domesticated type in the open and subsequently describes the arrangement of genetic interactions that reveal how the original farmers modified the composition of a type flora through the means of introducing external genetic material into the gene pool of the receiving population.

Now we do have a genetic picture of the origins of agriculture, that is corroborated by a vast array of taxonomic cross-comparison studies. Research indicates that wild variety of cereals had been in use for over a thousand years across the northern reaches of the Levant in Tell Abu-Hureyra and Mureybet by 12,000 BP, and across the northwestern hillsides of the Zagros and the Anti-Taurus highlands in Hallan Cemi, Qermez Dere, M'lefaat and Chogha Golan since 11,500 BP. It is though at the heart of the Golden Triangle in Cafer Hoyuk that the earliest evidence of all domesticated types - einkorn wheat, emmer wheat and barley appear first. Technologies associated with domestication of wild crops are quickly disseminated in direction of the south to Cayonu and Nevali Cori by 10,000 BP as they fan out subsequently in an outstanding rate of diffusion across multiple neolithisation localities of the Near East.

The second category of inquiries are concerned with archaeogenetic analyses of faunal remains in order to discover the original birthplace for emergence of domesticated sheep, goat, cattle and pig. These studies have also provided a promising picture of the early farmers efforts in taming wild varieties of bovidae. Extensive set of results indicate that both sheep and goat were the first and the earliest of the domesticated type across the region. Wild forms of the noted were in comparison to the other

2.20

2.21

Figure 63. Burnt remains of charcoaled wheat recovered from an archaeological site are capable of revealing its age, the composition of inhabitants dietary intake and the nature of the taxa itself - domesticated or wild. Studying botanical remains of this kind alongside genetic analysis of their origin can shed light on a variety of circumstantial elements, such as the whereabouts of its area of origin and its relative contrast or similarity to the other assemblages of botanical remains obtained in relevant sites of a designated region.

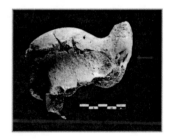

Figure 64. An auroch's humerus discovered in 2009 near the eastern corner of Enclosure D presents a tantalising case. The hunter's projectile is stuck near the frontal section of the beast's upper arm telling of a close miss. The shot was aimed at striking the beast's heart. Orientation of the projectile embedded indicates that the hunter stood as tall as the animal and had approached the beast from the right, with a distance of 10 to 40 meters. Animal remains of this sort can also tell us about the size of species and the genetic composition of them present at the vicinity of GobekliTepe.

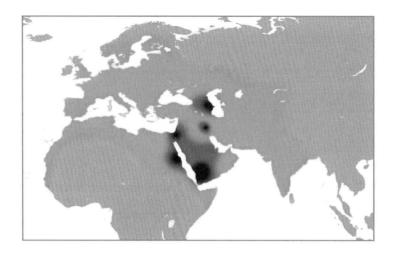

Figure 65. Distribution of Y-chromosome DNA haplogroup J-M304 or simply haplogroup J across the Near East, Asia, Europe and northern Africa. It is speculated that this haplogroup originated somewhat 40,000-30,000 years ago in Western Asia. Outside the Near East, carriers are found in significant numbers across Spain, Portugal, Italy, Greece, Cyprus and Albania. The haplogroup was divided into two main subclades, J-M267 and J-M172 respectively known as J1 and J2 subclades. Carriers of DNA haplogroup J comprised a majority of the Near Eastern population at the time of the Neolithic Revolution.

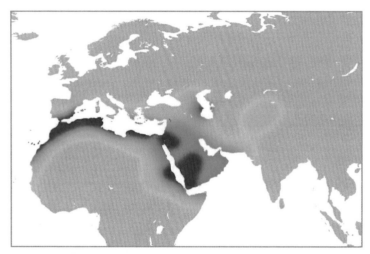

Figure 66. Distribution of haplogroup J-M267 or simply known J1 across the Near East, Asia, Europe and northern Africa. J1 is one of the main subclades of Y-chromosome DNA haplogroup J-M304, that is known as haplogroup J. The subclade is believed to have been originated during the terminal phase of the Last Glacial Maximum in Western Asia. Compared to its counterpart, subclade J2, haplogroup J1 is centred around georgraphical landscapes to the south of the Near East, particularly in Yemen, northern shorelines of Africa and the Sinai peninsula. It is also observed in high frequency near the horn of Africa and in southern Spain.

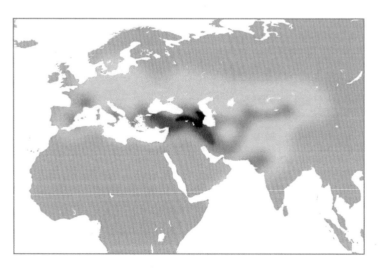

Figure 67. Distribution of haplogroup J-M172 or better known J2 across the Near East, Asia, Europe and northern Africa. J2 is one of the main subclades of Y-chromosome DNA haplogroup J-M304, that is known as haplogroup J. The subclade had emerged as a distinct haplogroup at around 18,000 BP in Western Asia. It is seen in highest frequency near the Caucasus and particularly across the arc of the Fertile Crescent, a favourable climatic zone that is the scene of the Neolithic Revolution. Carriers of haplogroup J2 are primarily centred through the northern landscape of the Near East, contrary to the carriers of J1 dominating the south.

taxa, much more manageable and docile. Contrary to the genetic studies of the founder crops that point out to the southern Anatolian landscape as the genesis of the domesticate types, current archaeogenetic consensus designate the northern hilly flanks of the Zagros as the origin of tamed wild sheep and goat. This happened at around 12,000 BP. The northwestern rocky shoulders of the Zagros alongside the highlands of southern Armenia and the eastern extension of the Anti-Taurus mountains are the only geographical areas in the Near East where wild indigenous family of short-haired mouflon, the ancestor of modern domesticated sheep could have been found in the open. The course of domestication is further pursued across the southern lowlands of the Anti-Taurus mountains in a narrow-sized convex of hills surrounding the opening of the Tigris and Euphrates. At this juncture, firstly wild boar and subsequently wild cattle are tamed by the advent of the 10,000 BP.

In a third category of studies, archaeogenetic analyses suggest a range of identifiable human migrations that could be detected alongside the diffusion of the Neolithic practices. Subclades of Y-chromosome DNA haplogroup J-M304 - generally described as J - are largely accredited as the original founders of agriculture and domestication of animals across the Near East. It appears that descendants of late glacial hunter-gatherers of the region carrying J-M172 marker - generally known as J2 - one of the main two sub-branches of haplogroup J, constituted a great majority of the inhabitants of the northern Near East and the Golden Triangle, concurrent to the emergence of the Neolithic practices across the domain. But in reality, the carriers of J-M172 or J2 subclade were not the only occupants of the immense landscape of the Near East during the Late Palaeolithic and PPN periods. Concentrated chiefly across the southern lowlands of the Near East, another subclade of haplogroup J bearing the marker J-M267 - commonly known as J1 - were also present in the lower latitudes when the Near East was at the cusp of the Neolithic revolution. By 12,000 BP, these populations had

Figure 68. Wild barley with the scientific name of hordeum spontaneum from PPN Chogha Golan in the foothills of the Zagros. Studies conducted by Riehl suggested that in Chogha Golan and at around 12,000 BP people were engaged in cultivating cereals, independent of the modes to be appearing across the Levant and southern Taurus ranges far away. In Chogha Golan, inhabitants cultivated wild barley, wheat, lentil and chickpeas and eventually domesticated emmer wheat during the course of the 11th and the 10th millennia BP.

Figure 69. Genetic studies on skeletal remains of an early farmer from Greece dating back to 7,500 years ago indicates a Near Eastern origin, hailing from the heart of the Fertile Crescent. Migrant farmers from the Near East were the driving force of the Neolithic Revolution across Europe.

2.22

2.23

already permeated into the interior of the Mesopotamian basin, converging with the carriers of the northern J2 subclade of the favourable agricultural horizon. In an additional genetic proliferation that could be traced back to the early Neolithic period of the region, farmers of the Golden Triangle carrying subclade J2 of haplogroup J appear to initiate a course of migration to the north through the Caucasus and through the western Anatolian landbridge across the Dardanelles. It is postulated that this migration had been spearheaded by the farmers of L212, one of the subclades of J2a. Another subclade of J2a described as J-M410 is believed to have been responsible for the spread of agricultural practices and domestication of wild species in southern Europe, through the corridor of eastern Mediterranean shorelines, Cyprus and southern Balkans.

# 3

## CHAPTER THREE

### GOBEKLI TEPE: THE STRUCTURE, RELIEFS AND ENVIRONS

## The World's Oldest Temple

Situated on the eastern termination of the Anti-Taurus ranges in southern Anatolia and located approximately 11 kilometers to the northeast of the city of Urfa - officially known as Sanliurfa - in southern Turkey, the pre-agricultural Neolithic site of Gobekli Tepe is more than 25 acres in expanse. The precise location of the site is characterised by UTM as 37S DB 93118 19633, Northing 4119631, Easting 493118 / 37°13'23.38"N - 38°55'20.75"E. The artificial hill consists of several knolls with depressions in between, preserving cultural remains of at least 21 circular or oval shaped enclosures, dating back to the 10th and 9th millennium BCE. The knolls are positioned on an elevation level of 779 meters above sea level and the mound has an almond-shaped plan, 427 meters above the adjoining plain of Harran to the south. The hill projects out of the limestone mountain bed in a southeasterly orientation of 22.8° west of north to 22.8° east of south. From atop the Gobekli hill, the horizon could be seen in nearly every direction.

Gobekli Tepe was constructed in the Terminal Late Palaeolithic period of the Near East, concomitant to the initial emergence of elementary Pre-pottery Neolithic communities across the Golden Triangle. The people undertaking this massive project were inhabitants of the mountain ranges of the southern Anti-Taurus chain, in a transitory stage in time that witnessed the abandonment of hunting and foraging ways of living on account of the emergence of agrarian lifestyle. The temple-structures of the site were constructed hundreds of years before the invention of pottery and six thousand years prior to the advent of writing. For these peculiar characteristics, Gobekli Tepe is renowned as the masterpiece of the pre-agricultural times. The people of Gobekli Tepe not only eyed the transition of socio-cultural norms to the favour of agricultural societies, they also witnessed an incredible breakthrough in the nature of religious beliefs. They beheld a revolutionary changeover from adherence to tribal

3.1

3.2

63

Figure 70. The Gobekli hill from the southeast. The artificial mound is seen over the limestone bedrock. The man-made tepe is about twenty meters higher than the average elevation of the hill. Archaeological trenches are laid out to the southwestern and northwestern segments of the hill. The artificial hill is easily distinguishable from the surrounding limestone bedrock, particularly as it presents a dramatic change in depositional sediments colour and it demonstrates a clear bulging outward. The mulberry tree indicates the direction of north.

Figure 71. The plain of Harran as seen from atop the Gobekli hill. The hill would have provided the hunter gatherers of antiquity with a panoramic view of the landscape. From over the Gobekli Tepe ridge, they were able to observe migration of animals, organise for a hunting campaign and oversee patterns of change in vegetation cover across the region. The hill is situated in the innermost depth of a U shaped region capable of attracting wild species of fauna into the interior of the terrain. For escaping the region, there existed a single way out to the south which could have been guarded effectively by the hunters gatherers, presenting excellent opportunities for entrapping and killing the wild.

convictions into the acceptance of large-scale regional systems of belief. Long before the emergence of the earliest civilisations in human history, the temple-site of Gobekli Tepe stood at the heart of a region that initiated the cultural transition from a familial perception of life to collective social undertakings, intra-regional interactions and communal modes of religion.

## Gobekli Tepe's Topography

Physical aspects of both natural and artificial components of the Gobekli hill are some of the most interesting features of the site. Temple sanctuaries are constructed over the tip of a large-scale limestone ridge known as Gobekli (Potbelly) that runs parallel to the Dagetegi mountain in the southwest and Kengerli ridge that is positioned to the northeast - both with a southeasterly orientation. The limestone bedrock of Gobekli Tepe, a landmark noticeable from miles away is 4.8 kilometers long and less than a kilometer wide. The bedrock is easily accessible through an opening to the west that constitutes a continuous and gradual downward ramp of descent.

3.3

Over the central prominence of the limestone bedrock, adjacent to the western opening, the people of Gobekli Tepe had constructed numerous successive complexes of enclosures, side by side - making use of basic devices of the Terminal Late Palaeolithic tool-kit such as microliths, hammers and chisels. Today, these enclosures form an artificial man-made mound that rises over 15 meters above the original limestone ridge. It provides a convenient viewpoint towards the lowland plains of Harran valley to the south. From atop this tepe, one could see the migration of animals, the movement of native species, and the plains of wild wheat and barley, stretching over across the horizon.

3.4

In favourable climatic conditions of the Terminal Late Palaeolithic period, large areas to the northern bank of the

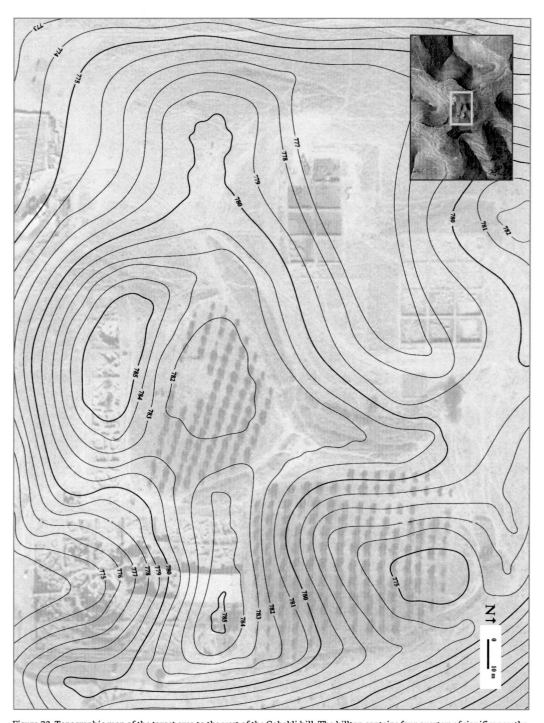

Figure 72. Topographic map of the target area to the west of the Gobekli hill. The hilltop contains four quarters of significance, the Suothwestern Depression, the Southwestern Mound, the Northwestern Depression and the Northwestern Mound. Changes in elevation level can provide the archaeologists with detailed knowledge of the knolls scattered across the hill, their shape and their position in relation to one another. The arrow points to the north.

Gobekli ridge were forested with trees and undergrowth, and towards the east and in the southerly orientation, the lowlands of the Syrian Jezirah were covered in pastures and wetlands. The Balikh Dihliz further to the south, hosted a well-supplied flush terrain of habitat, rich in biodiversity, containing all forms of animal life and naturally growing plants. Even today, the wild geese hover overhead in long skein of flights and bands of wild gazelle move past the Harran valley twice a year, reminiscent to the mass migrations of 11,000 years ago.

The Gobekli hill contains cultural remains associated with three phases of activity. We deliberately employ the term *activity* in an attempt to abstain from the use of terminologies such as *occupation* and *settlement* as those are loaded words with implications of a sedentary usage of the site. Archaeologists have not yet been able to discover material features corroborating

Figure 73. Aerial photography of Gobekli Tepe from north, prior to the beginning of excavations in 1995. The quality of soil atop hill is evidently different than the limestone ridge beneath. To the right of the aerial shot, a downward slope of limestone extension is seen, from which the access to the top of the hill could have been made possible in antiquity. The limestone mound beneath the man-made structures provided the people of Gobekli Tepe with building material suitable for quarrying T-shaped pillars and creating stone slabs, portholes, containers and figurines.

domestic modes of operation across the hill - i.e. hearths, kilns, storage pits, architectural elements confirming agrarian life or burials - the presence of which or lack thereof will be discussed in the coming chapters. Underneath the three layers of activity, the original bedrock level is laid that up to this point in time has been incapable of producing evidence of human interaction. As Gobekli Tepe is situated chronologically in a period in time where the initial move towards agriculture and domestication of the wild had begun - although intermittently - across the region and to the interior of the Golden Triangle, the first phase of activity across the site is chiefly dated to the initial Pre-pottey Neolithic period. This is ought to be accepted with a large caveat indicating that the people of Gobekli Tepe may or may not have known anything about the initial Neolithic practices of the day. Therefore, as the earliest phase of activity across the site is concurrent to a handful of Pre-pottery Neolithic settlements of the region, for all practical purposes, this lowermost level is considered to be belonging to the same archaeological phase. The three levels bearing cultural remains indicative of human interaction across the site are all positioned atop the bedrock. These consist of a Pre-pottery Neolithic A (PPNA) layer, that is generally described as Level III site-over. A younger phase of Pre-Pottery Neolithic B (PPNB) - Level II - lies above the Level III. The uppermost layer and the closest to the outer surface, Level I contains cultural remains post-dating the original usage of the site such as backfill and evidence of further activities concerned with post-Neolithic presence. The term Pre-pottery Neolithic is originated to distinguish continuous management of the Neolithic period across a site to namely; in prior to and after the invention of *farming (Neolithic)*, and in prior to and after the invention of *pottery (Pre-pottery)*. Gobekli Tepe does not contain evidence corroborating an archaeological phase of Pottery Neolithic activities - that is, it predates the invention of pottery.

3.6

Figure 74. Balikh river to the south of the Harran plain. The region, falling right in the centre of the Syrian Jezirah was strikingly complex in biodiversity, hosting all forms of animal and plant resources, birds, water and marine life. Furthermore the region is particularly significant as it borders farthest extensions of the Tigris and Euphrates near the upper Mesopotamian basin, where wild species of cattle and pig could be found in antiquity.

Figure 75. Domestic structure of a PPN space from Jericho in the Levant. The settlement holds a significant place in archaeology of the Late Palaleolithic and PPN of the Near East, as the crux of the earliest studies in the 20th century were focused on architectural and material characteristics of this settlement as a type-site. Studies conducted on Jericho by Kenyon paved the way for a better understanding of PPNA period from PPNB and the Pottery Neolithic era. Distinctions are paramount in architecture - circular, oval-shaped or rectilinear forms of houses, the use of mudbrick or lack thereof and generic shapes of storage spaces and hearths.

Figure 76. James Henrey Breasted was an American historian and archaeologist. He is considered to be the founder of the scientific field of egyptology. In this photograph dated to 1906 Breasted is seen with his family at the Temple of Karnak.

Figure 77. Ancient Times, A History of the Early World was penned down by Breasted in 1916. The term Fertile Crescent was framed by Breasted to designate a favourable arc across the Near East, suitable for practices of agriculture and domestication of animals. Breasted's Fertile Crescent stretched out further beyond the bounds of the Near Eastern archaeology into the depth of the Nile valley, where he believed the easrliest civilisations had originated from, concurrent to the communities of the Mesopotamian basin.

## A Short History of the Near Eastern Archaeological Studies

Klaus Schmidt had once described to the author of this book that "all fundamental steps in human history" have been taken in a terrain across the ancient Near East that is now known as the Fertile Crescent. Although this may appear to be a reductionist proposition, the assertions of the German archaeologist contain valid premises of scientific extrapolation. Schmidt in fact was not the only modern archaeologist postulating claims of Near Eastern origins for certain breakthroughs in the emergence of human civilisation. Over a hundred years earlier, James Henry Breasted the renowned egyptologist of the time, introduced the term Fertile Crescent in a book titled *Ancient Times, A History of the Early World*, to describe a crescent shaped region that he concluded to be the cradle of the early human development. Material and physical evidence unearthed across the region had been for long, and are yet in support of the assertions made by Breasted. The hypothetical boundaries of the Fertile Crescent that the late egyptologist stamped out, stretches from the riverine shores of the Nile, out to the northern plains of Syria, southern regions of Turkey and western borders of Iran. The first farming communities, the first evidence of writing, the earliest towns, the earliest codes of law, and the oldest inventions in pottery all arose in this hypothetical terrain. In previous chapters, we have extensively expounded on the significance of the ancient Near East and the positioning of the Golden Triangle in the core region of the Fertile Crescent.

3.7

For years, the study of the Fertile Crescent was chiefly focused on the *Levantine* corridor - a terminology of Italian origin, denoting *the east* where the rising sun casted its shining rays above the farthermost shores of the Mediterranean Sea. Among all the localities of the Fertile Crescent, the Levant was the focus of studies for many centuries prior to the advent of modern science of archaeology, in part due to the richness of written

3.8

ancient records - mainly Biblical - explaining its past people and civilisations and more importantly as a result of the long lasting Judeo-Christian conviction of the Holy Land viewed as the centre of the world. A rational conclusion of the sort had entailed a proviso that all that existed in the world, had to have emerged from the land of the Levant.

Unmoved by the burden of religious sentiments, modern anthropologists and archaeologists of the twentieth century, pursued an objective and methodological approach in their study of the Fertile Crescent and its material remains. In this period, the region of the Levant was yet an impressive target for archaeological studies, as the wealth of physical remains throughout the landscape was unduly spellbinding. A pervasive view had existed in time, perpetuating a normative idealisation - that in this part of the Fertile Crescent, continuous flourishing cultures had existed in antiquity, in an uninterrupted sequence. The question to be asked in response was a simple one, what about the rest of the region? And the rest of the region at the time had remained for all practical purposes, unexplored.

Across the Levant and in Jericho, one of the most influential archaeologists of the twentieth century, Kathleen Kenyon, had emerged as a tireless advocate the Levantine precedence. Her ceaseless efforts, although narrowly focused on the archaeology of the Levantine margin, laid the groundwork for future research and scientific initiatives - chiefly aimed at understanding the nature of Neolithic transition across the entire region. In the following decades, the attention was gradually shifted towards the northern Mesopotamian plains of Tigris and Euphrates, where many unveiled cities and settlements were subjected to intensive and large-scale seasonal excavations. The leading figure in this paradigm shift was Robert Braidwood of the University of Chicago, one of the founders of modern scientific archaeology. In the course of studies conducted across the entirety of the Near Eastern theatre, it was determined that many

3.9

Figure 78. Kathleen Kenyon at Jericho, 1964. Kenyon was a distinguished Biblical scholar and director of the British Museum. She was one of the leading British archaeologists engaged in excavations at Jericho where she presented a distinct stratigraphic analysis of the PPN Near Eastern period.

Figure 79. Robert John Braidwood (standing third from right) alongside members of the team of archaeologists from the University of Chicago, Oriental Institute. In 1963, Braidwood embarked on a trip to the Middle East, with the aim of studying the earliest human settlements along the coastlines of Tigris and Euphrates rivers. He later expanded his campaign towards north in southern Turkey, Iraqi Kurdistan and the western Iranian Zagros. The team of archaelogists led by Braidwood in collaboration with local archaeological institutes were the first to provide records of all Near Eastern sites.

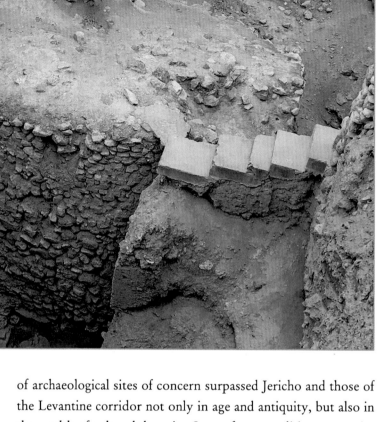

Figure 80. Cultural remains of a round PPNA tower-shaped structure from Jericho in the Levant excavated by Kathleen Kenyon. The stone structure is 11 meters high and 7 meters wide. It dates back to the 10th millennium BP. The structure contains an internal passage with staircases made of limestone that run diagonal to the height of the tower and provide access to top of the building from a much lower entrance. The quality of the building indicates it was the work of a people with long tradition of masonry.

of archaeological sites of concern surpassed Jericho and those of the Levantine corridor not only in age and antiquity, but also in the wealth of cultural deposits. Soon after, expeditionary parties from major oriental institutes and universities of the world were catapulted to the region, combing through every inch of the Fertile Crescent, in various landscapes of southern Turkey, northern Iraq and Syria and western Iran. Preliminary reports of archaeological surveys were presented in voluminous records, delivered by the acclaimed Turkish archaeologist Mrs. Halet Çambel from the University of Istanbul and Robert Braidwood himself. Hilly Flanks hypothesis ventured by the University of Chicago project, postulated the rocky fringes of the Taurus and the Zagros mountains as birthplaces of farming and animal husbandry. These were hundreds of miles distant from the well-

3.10

known Levantine apex. The accounts predicted these terrains will soon would be found to be the cradle of Neolithic Revolution. The natural habitat, running rivers, pluvial plains, distribution of wild species of animals and plants, and the overall ecological conditions of the area, along with the results of paleo-botanical analyses, all foretold the story of a Golden Triangle in which the Neolithic way of life should have been begun. A new age in archaeological studies of the region had begun.

## The Discovery of Gobekli Tepe

A team of German archaeologists from the University of Heidelberg was assigned by the Turkish authorities in 1979 to conduct a salvage operation on Nevali Cori - a Neolithic settlement on the banks of the Euphrates river dating to over 10,550 years ago. Construction of the colossal embankment - officially known as the Ataturk Dam had begun the year before, and hydraulic studies had precisely predicted that the artificial reservoir created in the wake of Ataturk's completion would generate a substantial rise in Euphrates echelon, inundating the Neolithic settlement and the plains adjacent to the site. Upon arrival in Turkey in 1982, German archaeologists under the lead of Harald Hauptmann conducted 8 seasonal rescue operations at the site spanning from 1982 to 1992. Excavations unearthed numerous architectural structures, houses, hearths, communal buildings, burial pits and remains of multiple sanctuaries to the west and the northwestern hilly flanks of the site. The temples were sources of wonder and amazement, with large rectangular enclosures, surrounded by T-shaped pillars on all sides, complemented in the centre by anthropromorphic monoliths positioned in limestone pedestal bases.

The placement of hydraulic fill into the dike section of the Ataturk Dam in 1992 brought the Nevali Cori project to its near end. The result of studies had been published concurrent to the course of excavations by Hauptmann in the journal of Anatolian

3.11

Figure 81. Temple structure to the southwest of the PPN and Neolithic settlement of Nevali Cori. One of the central pillars is remained in-situ with the upper segment broken in half. The pillar is persumed to have a T-shape form and it contains reliefs of arms and fingers engraved similar to the anthropromorphic monoliths of Gobekli Tepe. The temple structure and the settlement to the east of the mound were excavated by Harald Hauptman in the 1980s.

Figure 82. Aerial photograph of the enormous artificial lake created as a result of the construction of Ataturk Dam (right hand side of the photograph). The inundation of Eurphrates due to the building of a series of dams has resulted in the submergence of a dozen important archaeological sites alongside the river shoreline, including Jerf el-Ahmar, Mureybet and Nevali Cori.

Figure 83. Microliths appear in abundance over the surface of the hill in and around Gobekli Tepe. Stone tools were the main technological devices that were utilised by the hunter gatherers of antiquity in creating the temple structures of Gobekli Tepe. They were in addition used in the course of hunting, feasting and activities of everyday life.

Figure 84. Klaus Schmidt, one of the leading members of the German archaeological team in southern Turkey, examines lithics unearthed at Nevali Cori's communal building 1988. As a senior archaeologist, Schmidt had gained a clear understanding of Nevali Cori's geographical, regional and cultural significance. Working alongside Harald Hauptmann for years, provided him with a wealth of experience and insight that contributed to the discovery of Gobekli Tepe at last.

Studies from 1981 to 1994 and artefacts unearthed, including the lower section of an anthropomorphic pillar had been put on exhibition at the Sanliurfa Museum of Archaeology. Although, the salvage project had terminated in an abrupt manner, large-scale excavations at Nevali Cori had attracted attention of a large group of archaeologists concerned with the Neolithic studies of the Near East. The mysteries of Nevali Cori's enclosed sanctuaries, ceremonial houses with interconnected underfloor channels and their concealed anti-chambers, figurines of meticulous detail and its mortar coated walls remained alive in the hearts and minds of the researchers engaged. One of those, Klaus Schmidt - a prominent member of the Hauptmann's team - ventured into the surrounding landscape, treading on the heels of archival records provided by the joint team of Çambel and Braidwood decades before, in hope of discovering a long forgotten Neolithic settlement across the region.

3.12

In the summer of 1993, Schmidt came upon the site of Gobekli Tepe, trailing on the path of a list of potential archaeological sites, sought after by Peter Benedict earlier, one of the archaeological surveyors of the University of Chicago in 1963. The notes, accounted for the site, described it as a "complex of round-topped knolls of red earth" dominated by "small cemeteries". It is open to question whether Benedict had ever set foot on the tip of the mount, or else he would have been able to take note of lithic littered hilltop. Schmidt on the other hand had noticed the particular dome-shaped profile of the artificial section in sight. This could have not been a natural tepe by any stretch of imagination and the German archaeologist was urged to believe that the mound was of a PPN nature, simply because he was not able to locate any shards of pottery on the surface. After he was led to the top of the mound by a Kurdish middle-aged shepherd named Savak Yildiz, which recounted the experience as "hurried" and Schmidt's excitement upon noticing numerous flints scattered close to the ground surface as "thrilling", Schmidt returned to Urfa where he was stationed at

3.13

the time - entertaining no doubt that he had set foot upon a remarkable find. This was the discovery of his lifetime. He was yet holding the original notes of Peter Benedict in hand, which he had previously copied down of the archival records. The proposed dating section of the profile read "A possible Byzantine cemetery" - an erroneous wrong that Schmidt was determined to make right.

## Excavations at Gobekli Tepe

Limestone quarries of the Gobekli ridge were intended to be used as foundation ballast and gravel, furnishing the new Urfa to Mardin highway that was in the midst of construction in 1992. Klaus Schmidt was confident of the wealth of the cultural remains beneath the surface of the mound, but at this juncture he had ought to be swift and decisive in promoting the significance of his newly discovered site. The German Archaeological Institute based in Istanbul considered the matter with utmost urgency and further correspondence between the institution and the Turkish authorities proved to be one of the critical tools in establishing effective means of obtaining mutual endowments to subsidise the project. In early 1994, over a year and a half after the discovery of the hill by Schmidt, the German archaeologist returned to the site with a team of five researchers. Original

Figure 85. One of the central pillars of Nevali Cori's temple with the upper segment missing (right). Note the positioning of arms along the side profiles and the fingers to the front. Two rows of parallel lines appear on both sides of the front face, stretching from top to the bottom right above the waist line. An aerial photograph of the Nevali Cori's sanctuary, decorated with terrazzo flooring (left). Notice the double enclosing wall to the east and the benches incorporated into the interior boundaries of strucure. The opening is envisioned from south with steps leading down to the main floor of the enclosure, that is strikingly in an evident rectangular form - indication of its belonging to the PPNB period. The base of the missing central pillar was examined through a sondage dug deep beneath the platform which resulted in discovery of a human crania and cultural remains indicating burial. The original structure had fourteen pillars around the periphery and two in the centre, all but three are missing.

Figure 86. The first trench laid out to the western extension of the Southwestern Depression at Gobekli Tepe. Excavation of the set of trenches to the Southwestern Depression were complemented by concurrent work over the Southwestern Mound.

Figure 87. One of the fascinating aspects of finds at Gobekli Tepe is the presence of benches around the interior of enclosing walls. The feature, previously observed by archaeologists conducting research at Nevali Cori not only indicates a close resemblance in architectural characteristics of the two sites, but may also indicates a particular engineering feat that made the builders capable of providing a stable footing for peripheral T-shaped pillars. Indications of interment beneath the benches at Nevali Cori, persuaded Schmidt to postulate the Gobekli Tepe's benches too might have burial digs beneath them. A theory that had not yet been supported by cultural evidence.

surface surveys were conducted in an attempt to outline the physical boundaries of the knolls positioned over the hill and their exact placement across the site. The following summer, a comprehensive geomagnetic survey was performed in conjunction with ground-penetrating radar studies, detailing the proximity and the size of underground architectural features. Schmidt's companions had noticed that over the southern tip of the ridge, the evidence of human impact was rather remarkable in comparison to the other areas of the mound. The physical properties of the hill were not concealed from the eyes of a team of experienced and adept excavators. Geophysical results at this contingent indicated the presence of over 200 pillars underground, interspersed across more than 21 circular zones. When the archaeological team added multiple areas recently found, to the original plan of excavations, the site appeared in its full enormity and size. The first trenches were laid to the southwest of the artificial mound in a region described as the southwestern mound in 9 by 9 square meters of surface grid. Soon after this, the team began to expand the scope of excavations to the adjacent section of the hill commonly known as the southwestern depression, digging out multiple pillars of Enclosure A. Intrusive excavations continued in the summer of 1996 in collaboration with the German Archaeological Institute (Deutsches Archaeologisches Institut) and the Urfa Archaeology Museum of Turkey. Trenches were expanded across the entire hill and further to the west of a mulberry tree revered by the locals as an object of well-wishes and offerings - a good omen.

For intrusive excavations, the German Archaeological team narrowed the scope of examinations to four distinct spaces atop the hill. These were the Southwestern Depression, the Southwestern Mound, the Northwestern Depression and the Northwestern Mound. Trenches of the Southwestern Mound were the foremost quarters of the site examined by the archaeologists. From the beginning of 1997 and near the

3.14

Figure 88. Aerial photography of the first set of trenches over the Southwestern Depression in 1996, with Enclosure A in the centre, with pillars 1, 2, 3, 4 and 5 appearing evident. Further excavations later were picked up from the northern (right hand side) of the initial dig.

Figure 89. The four main areas of interest over the Gobekli hill. The Northwestern Mound and the Northwestern Depression are seen to the north of the hill, while the Southwestern Mound and the Southwestern Depression could be seen near the centre. The Southwestern Depression is considered to be the main area of excavation at the site, yeilding Enclosures A, B, C, D and G and the Lion pillar building. The mulberry tree to the top right hand side corner of the area indicated direction of north.

southern extension of the Southwestern Depression - adjacent to the initial set of digs - a number of large limestone pillars arranged in semi-circular and circular spaces of different sizes were unearthed - enclosures known today as A and B. It soon became clear that the peripheral pillars were often complemented with a pair of much larger in size monoliths standing in the centre - much like the familiar arrangement observed previously at Nevali Cori. In some cases, boundaries of enclosures appeared in a rectangular plan rather than precise circular form. This dichotomy of shape in either architectural patterns of enclosures, in the absence of a clear stratigraphic understanding of the site, proved to be a rather puzzling feature of the site at the outset. The initial reading of the enclosures uncovered indicated that temple structures of Gobekli Tepe were built in two distinct periods of time - perhaps a majority of larger enclosure in circular patterns belonging to the PPNA

3.15

period and the rectangular structures belonging to the the distinct PPNB time.

The excavation team followed a system of numbering for exposed pillars that followed the order of their discovery. Enclosures on the other hand were labeled in alphabetic order. Work at trenches of Enclosure A were began in 1995 and the semi-circular structure was subsequently excavated for 3 consecutive years. Enclosure B appeared in early 1998 followed by its adjacent ring of Enclosure C the same winter. For the next 5 years, Klaus Schmidt and the team of archaeologists at Gobekli Tepe centred their attention towards these three enclosures. In 1999, 2001 and 2002, preliminary reports were published outlining features of the site, detailed analysis of its enclosures, their pillars and motifs. A temporary cover was constructed over the enclosures A and B in 2002. Enclosure C on the other hand, had remained semi-excavated at the time, particularly in light of high quantities of pillars discovered, the enormous size of the enclosure and the amount of backfill that was thrown into the deep structure in antiquity, at the time of its abandonment. Excavations at this enclosure continued all the way to the year 2008. The last of the main structures unearthed at the site, Enclosure D was discovered in 2001. Scooping out the remains of this enclosure has proven to be one of the most painstaking tasks undertaken at the site. This was the largest enclosure across Gobekli Tepe yet to be discovered, and it contained the most sizeable T-shaped pillars at the site. Enclosure D is also the oldest, the deepest in stratigraphic position and the most preserved of all structures unearthed. Excavating this structure took over ten years of intense archaeological work. Concurrent to the excavation of the southwestern depression, the work across the other three main areas of interest were also in continuation. The trenches dug out to the Southwestern Mound were complemented by structural finds appearing over the Northwestern Mound and subsequently trenches of the Northwestern Depression. Architectural features of these spaces

3.16

Figure 90. Enclosure B, view from northwest during the course of excavations. The enclosure initially was overflown with the fill that covered the central T-shaped pillars and the pillars around the periphery. The sanctuary was fully buried under the deposition. This in turn had been a significant factor in preservation of the site and its architectural features, protecting the sanctuary beneath layers of rock, sediments, faunal remains, lithics and dump.

Figure 91. Enclosure D during the course of excavations, view from west. The central pillars weighing over 40 tonnes on average were secured using traditional mechanical principles, similar to the methods used in antiquity by the nuter gatherers of Gobekli Tepe to put them in place. The two central pillars were both leaning sideways against the backfill the was laid in the space between the two, therefore the noted fill was the last segment of the Enclosure's interior to be explored by the archaeologists.

| Enclosure | Discovery | Excavation Period | Level | Major length in m | Minor length in m | Area and shape | Boundary type | Number and list of pillars excavated | Dominant features |
|---|---|---|---|---|---|---|---|---|---|
| A | 1995 | 1996-1997 | Directly under the backfill - Level III | 7.9 | 7.1 | Semi-rectangular plan with a single crescent shaped side 44 sqm | Single | 5 pillars: 1-2-3-4-5- possibly 17 | At Southwestern Depression. Loam and cobbles flooring. |
| B | 1998 | 1998-2002 | Directly under the backfill - Level III | 9.5 | 8.4 | Oval shaped 62 sqm | Single | 9 pillars: 6-7-8-9-10-14-15-1 6-34 | At Southwestern Depression. Concrete like waterproof terrazzo floor. |
| C | 1998 | 1998-2008 | Directly under the backfill - Level III | Interior (11.2) Exterior (17.1) | Interior (9.2) Exterior (14.6) | Oval shaped Interior (73 sqm) Exterior (196 sqm) | Double | 19 pillars: 11-12-13-23-24-25-26-27-28-29-35-36-37-39-40-44-45-46-47 | Positioned to the east of Enclosure B at Southwestern Depression. Well smoothed bedrock as floor |
| D | 2001 | 2002-2012 | Directly under the backfill - Level III | Interior (14.8) Exterior (20.6) | Interior (10.6) Exterior (14.3) | Oval shaped Interior (123 sqm) Exterior (231 sqm) | Single - Partly Double walled to the south | 13 pillars: 18-19-20-21-22-30-31-32-33-38-41-42-43 | Positioned to the north of Enclsoure C at the Southwestern Depression. Well smoothed bedrock for flooring |
| E | 1995 | 1995-1996 | Uncertain | 9.6 | 9.5 | Oval shaped 91 sqm | Single | 2 pillars | At Northwestern Mound |
| F | 1997 | 1997 | Uncertain | 10.1 | 9.2 | Circular 92.9 sqm | Single | 8 pillars: XXIII, XXIV, XXV, XXVI, XXXIV, XXXV, XXXVI, XXXVII | At Southwestern Mound |
| G | 2001 | 2001- 2002 | Uncertain | 8.6 | 7.8 | Oval shaped 67 sqm | Single | 2 pillars: XXII, XLIII | Positioned to the west of Enclosure D |
| Lion Pillar Building | 1998 | 1998-1999 | Level II | 7.1 | 5.3 | Rectangular 39.7 | Single | 6 pillars: I, II, III, IV, V, VI | Positioned to the north of the Southwestern Depression, adjacent to the mulberry tree |

Figure 92. Table describing enclosures year of discovery, period of excavation, stratigraphic layer, size, area, the number of pillars discovered and dominant features. The table is based on unearthed cultural remains by 2017.

exposed, indicate a Neolithic occupation of the site that is although non-domestic, it corroborates the presence of a population in the vicinity of the temple site who were engaged in construction of the sanctuaries.

By 2012, excavations had uncovered over 4,046 square meters, and as Schmidt once unsurprisingly reminded me, this "only covered about 5 per cent of the totality of the site". All the four sanctuaries were located on top of the southern slope, in a near proximal distance to one another - often brushing against each other's outer boundaries. As expounded before, among the four chief enclosures, the enclosure D has been the largest and the best preserved so far. This enclosure in particular, provides a window of opportunity to understand the authentic architectural composure of the sanctuaries in antiquity, seldom found as intact as those of the Enclosure D anywhere else across the hill. At this enclosure, the position of the two central pillars at the heart of the oval shaped segment is distinguishably clear. The central pillars are surrounded by T-shaped limestone slabs, precisely 12 of them, which are of a relatively smaller size.

3.17

## Stratigraphic Composition of the Southwestern Depression

The form of the Southwestern Depression as a grading slope has been modified by human activity in antiquity and erosion at a relatively later stage in time. In total, four distinct Levels of remains have been recognised across the mound, associated with three levels. The oldest level belongs to the PPNA era, where T-shaped pillars stand in oval shaped enclosures dating back to about 10,000 BCE. Beneath this layer, a continuous strata of limestone bedrock exists that has not been able to provide any remains associated with intensive human activity or presence at the site. We can clearly consider this lowermost layer as the bedrock limestone. In contrast, to the north of the PPNA level - officially known as Level III - an intermediary sequence is seen which contains rectangular structures. Sanctuaries of this layer,

Figure 93. The statue of a boar discovered alongside two ground stones near the base of the central pillars at Enclosure C. The arrow indicates north. These all have been recovered from loads of backfill that covered them, indicating that their configuration conveys a pruposeful message with symbolic meaning. The meal grinds are about half a meter in diameter and the boar statue is about 30 centimeters long.

Figure 94. Terrazzo flooring of Enclosure C. The terrazzo is made of burnt limestone and clay and it is impenetrable to moisture and very durable. Structures with terrazzo flooring have been discovered at Jericho, Nevali Cori and Cayonu. The material feat was an invention of the PPN period of the Near East.

Figure 95. Aerial photography of the Southwestern Despression. Enclosure A is situated to the southwest of the area with enclosures B and C to the north and the northwest of its boundaries. Enclosure D is positioned right in the centre. The Lion pillar building and its adjacent rectangular enclosure of PPNB period are covered in this photograph by the roofing to the north of the area. The mulberry tree again to the top right hand side indicated direction of north. The farthest trenches of the Southwestern Mound could also be seen near the left hand side centre of the figure.

show clear reduction in the size of pillars and enclosures are more than often smaller than the PPNA ones. This layer - described as Level II - belongs to the 9th millennium BCE of PPNB period, supraposed by a large horizon of backfill. The fill material creates a complex set of strata over the two levels of PPNA and PPNB origin, but no clear level of activity is assigned to this layer. Cultural remains of the backfill are often described to be on par with the PPN level to which they are thrown in, although in essence, whatever found in the backfill post-dates the original usage of the beneath PPN sanctuary. Ultimately a unique level of colluvial sediments to the south of the site is singled out as Level I. Cultural remains of this level are either redeposited sediments or they belong to the youngest and the uppermost sequence of Gobekli Tepe of a Roman or a later period.

3.18

At around 8,200 BCE the site was in its entirety abandoned and evidence for further activities over Gobekli Tepe only re-appear at around the timeframe of the pre-medieval period and modern era. Various hypotheses have been put forward in an attempt to explain the meaning and intention of this act of abandonment. Schmidt himself considered one of the most commonly accepted of all hypotheses, to be capable of explaining the cause. He postulated that the terminal people of Gobckli Tepe, had found the spiritual world of their ancestors exceedingly irrelevant to their newly adopted way of life. The abandonment coincides with the transition of the Near Eastern societies of hunter gatherers and sedentary contingents, into large-scale agrarian communities. Whilst there are clear common premises on the finds unearthed at Gobekli Tepe that help to explain the Neolithic transition, the consensus has yet to emerge describing how complex adaptations of the sort were implemented.

Figure 96. A 3-D recreation of the Southwestern Depression exhibited at Gobekli Tepe's visitor centre. The artefact demonstrates a cross-sectional view of the depression from the direction of west, showing enclosures C and D near the lower stratigraohic level of the site, followed immeiately by enclosures A and B to the lower right hand side corner of the piece. Notice the increase in elevation from south to north with later PPNB structures to the top left hand side corner of the piece appearing in rectangular form.

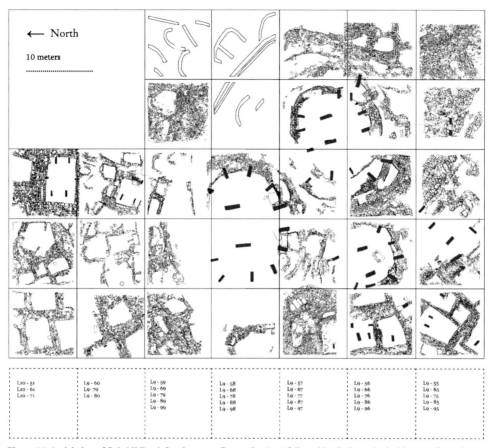

| L10 - 51<br>L10 - 61<br>L10 - 71 | L9 - 60<br>L9 - 70<br>L9 - 80 | L9 - 59<br>L9 - 69<br>L9 - 79<br>L9 - 89<br>L9 - 99 | L9 - 58<br>L9 - 68<br>L9 - 78<br>L9 - 88<br>L9 - 98 | L9 - 57<br>L9 - 67<br>L9 - 77<br>L9 - 87<br>L9 - 97 | L9 - 56<br>L9 - 66<br>L9 - 76<br>L9 - 86<br>L9 - 96 | L9 - 55<br>L9 - 65<br>L9 - 75<br>L9 - 85<br>L9 - 95 |

Figure 97. Aerial plan of Gobekli Tepe's Southwestern Depression (top) followed by the hypothetical layout of trenches (10x10 meters) and their labelling in dotted lines (centre). The cross-sectional profile of the Southwestern Depression (below) is shown with the current positioning of enclosures and their stratigraphic placement (lowermost figure).

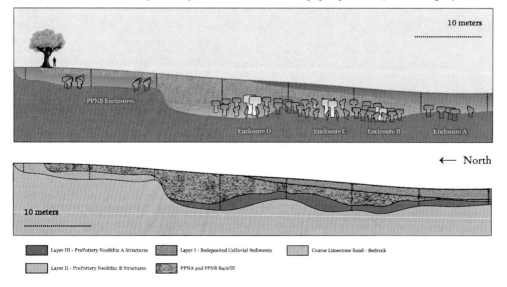

## Stratigraphic Analysis and Dating

Building history of enclosures is the subject of current studies by Katja Piesker of German Archaeological Institute. The result of this analysis which will be provided in the future will shed light on the sequence of construction activities, across the site in antiquity. In addition, a team of archaeologists under the direction of Tilman Muller and in coordination with the University of Karlsruhe, have been delegated for creating 3-D documentation of architectural remains discovered throughout the hill, which will contribute to the purpose of cross-comparing structural forms and their relative similarities or differences. Concurrent to these analyses, residue charcoals and debris of mulberry fruit, pistachio and fragments of branches have been unearthed in deep segments of Enclosures A, C and D beneath and adjacent to the pillars. Radiocarbon dating of these organic remains have fortunately yielded results that are capable of showing occupation dates across various enclosures. A piece of charcoal pistachio found in-situ near the ring walls of Enclosure D has provided an age of roughly 11,800 BP. Another charcoal remain from a fragment of a broken branch obtained from Enclosure C determines a timeframe of 11,650 years ± 30 years. Similar remains of charcoal discovered in Enclosure A, represent a later date of 11,500 ± 53 in support of previous speculation that had placed this enclosure among the younger category of sanctuaries. Radiocarbon dating results of 14 samples examined across the site corroborate architectural and archaeological hypotheses proposed in past. They suggest an older dates associated with larger and deeper enclosures and younger dates with respect to the semi-circular or rectangular sanctuaries of smaller size. In all cases, the results indicate a Pre-pottery Neolithic usage of the site and dates achieved through examination of the backfill prove the abandonment of structures in late 9th millennium BCE.

3.19

Figure 98. Composition of the fill through the profile of Enclosure E, view from south. Changes in coarsness, shape, colour and density of the remains (or backfill) may be indicative of stratigraphic changes. Parameters taken into account across the site vary from each quarter to the next. Apart from general stratigraphic composition of the Southwestern Depression, studies on chronological aspects of other areas have not been made yet available.

# 4

## CHAPTER FOUR

### THE T-SHAPED PILLARS

## T-shaped Pillars of Gobekli Tepe

In the absence of any remains demonstrating presence of storage spaces, hearths, burial pits or elements of domestic architecture, the importance of Gobekli Tepe's stone pillars appears to be fundamental to a satisfactory analysis of the site and the purpose that it served. At this moment, pillars are some of the most valuable remains discovered across the site that arc capable of providing us with a wide range of information. Information about the people of Gobekli Tepe, their communal beliefs, their network of regional communication with the rest of the settlements across the Near East and their technological advancements in the advent of PPN period. Gobekli Tepe's T-shaped pillars can be analysed with respect to four distinct areas of study; a) their significance in the context of their regional placement, b) stratigraphic context in which they have been discovered, c) their architectural importance across the site and in comparison to the other communal structures of the Near East, and finally d) their symbolic meanings.

Communal buildings are ubiquitous across the PPN and Neolithic settlements of the Near East. Concurrent to the occupation of Gobekli Tepe, they could be found in archaeological horizons of PPN Mureybet and Jerf el-Ahmar, closer to the Levantine corridor, Sheikh-e Abad in Iranian Zagros, and Cayonu and Nevali Cori throughout the Golden Triangle. At Mureybet and Jerf el-Ahmar, special purpose buildings of circular form have been discovered and studied by Stordeur. Stipulations of their function, indicate a usage of organic posts for the purpose of facilitating structural integrity of the buildings. Closer to the heart of the Golden Triangle though, at Cayonu and Nevali Cori respectively studied by Schirmer and Hauptmann, support for the roof covering was provided by the means of rock-cut pillars, synonymous to the architectural tradition of Gobekli Tepe. These are always positioned at around inner boundaries of sanctuaries and in some cases are

4.1

Figure 99. Reliefs over the shaft of the eastern central pillar of Enclosure D. The pillar stands 5.5 meters tall. The arms engraved on its lateral profiles end above the waist line over the frontal surface of the pillar. The anthropromorphic figure's belt is seen decorated with various symbols. Its fingers are in addition shown with meticulous details. What is distinctively unqiue with respect to the central pillars at Gobekli Tepe, is the relief of a loincloth made out of a fox hide that is worn covering the groins and the frontal segment of the being, indicative of a community engaged in hunting the wild for sustenance.

complemented by a pair of stone pillars in the centre, analogous to Gobekli Tepe's mode of architecture. The most important settlement of the sort to be excavated with similar architectural features to Gobekli Tepe, was Nevali Cori. Resemblances of Nevali Cori's sanctuaries and those of Gobekli Tepe are striking. In the two, pillars were quarried out of single bulk of limestone rock, and are curiously shaped in T forms. Central pillars in both communities were constructed - stylised as humanlike beings - with carvings of arms engraved over the flat sides of the profiles. Pillars of the Nevali Cori communal buildings - from both stratigraphic layers of Levels II and III - were of a much smaller size in comparison to the T-shaped pillars of Gobekli Tepe, but similar to the central pillars of Enclosures B, C and D, they were positioned in the base limestone bed over a single thin layer of terrazzo. Nevali Cori's

4.2

central pillars were also carved exhibiting detailed fingers to the front of the shaft, which appear directly over the waist segment of the anthropomorphic post. Similarities and contrasts of the two sites will be explored later in this chapter. Let us now focus on stratigraphic context within which T-shaped pillars have been unearthed at Gobekli Tepe.

T-shaped pillars have been discovered across all four main areas of excavation at Gobekli Tepe. In Southwestern Depression, T-shaped pillars have been exposed in both PPNA - Level III - and PPNB - Level II - phases of occupation. In both rectangular and oval-shaped sanctuaries, pillars are the most common type of structural elements across the depression. They are witnessed in enclosures A, B, C, D, G and over the Lion Pillar Building and its adjacent rectangular sanctuary to the south. Over the Southwestern Mound, Enclosure F has been uncovered with the presence of T-shaped pillars in the context of an intermediate phase, uncertain from an stratigraphic point of view, which does nevertheless fall into a chronological horizon belonging to either PPNA or PPB period. Over the northwestern extensions of the site, remains of T-shaped pillars have been found at a remote sanctuary known as Enclosure E. In all these cases, pillars present a T-shape form and never appear in any other stylistically divergent appearance.

With respect to their architectural characteristics, most pillars appear to have an average height of 3 to 4 meters. The central pillars, larger in size than those around the periphery are always taller - some well over 5.5 meters. Enclosure A has yielded 5 pillars so far and enclosures B, C and D, are respectively comprised of 9, 19 and 13 pillars. With the Southwestern Mound in mind, Enclosure F has presented 8 T-shaped pillars up to this point, with further two pillars potentially hidden in the trenches adjacent to the north. Over the northwestern extension of the hill, Enclosure E contains pedestal remains of two upright pillars removed in antiquity. In short, Enclosure C with 17 pillars

4.3

4.4

Figure 100. One of the Nevali Cori's central pillars containig reliefs of arms and fingers synonymous to the central pillars of Gobekli Tepe. Notice the parallel strips along the opposite lengths of the frontal segment.

Figure 101. Enclosure C, one of the larger temple structures of Gobekli hill contains the highest number of pillars in two distinct rings of surrounding walls. Nevertheless, the enclosure was severly damaged in antiquity, particularly at the time of its abandonment where it was filled up with backfill, comprising of dirt, animal remains, boulders and lithics. In this photograph one of the central pillars of enclosure is shown broken in three pieces, with the highest segment missing. The other matching central pillar is in worse condition, with simply the base to be the only preserved component of it.

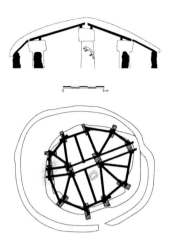

Figure 102. Hypothetical reconstruction of the roofing over the central area of Enclosure B. The wooden platform atop the central pillars would have provided the organically constructed beams adjacent with a framework which in turn was linked up to the upper surface segment of the pillars around the periphery, all in cohesion and supported by long timber boards.

Figure 103. Reliefs of a boar and a predator (possibly a fox) carved beneath a band of ducks. Notice the highly prominent canine teeth of the wild boar, purposefully distinguished as a male species alongside a matching figure of a panting fox.

dispersed around two rings of enclosing walls and 2 larger central pillars in the middle, has the highest number of pillar posts across the site. Unfortunately the unearthed architectural and stylistic components of this enclosure are particularly problematical and are severely damaged. Enclosure D on the other hand, contains the most preserved set of pillars discovered yet, and the highest number of T-shaped pillars on the periphery and in one single ring of enclosing walls.

There appears to be an additional usage to the shape of the pillars across the site. These architectural features, not only functioned as mediums, delivering us stories from the life and times of the people of Gobekli Tepe, but they also contain carefully designed structures that shed light on their collective performance across the site. Fourteen of the surrounding pillars unearthed so far, demonstrate deep depression cuts parallel or perpendicular to the uppermost surface of their head segments. These incisions may served as static footings for the beams that in antiquity supported roof coverings of each distinct sanctuary. If sanctuaries were roofed, archaeologists have not been able to get hold of architectural remains indicative of the nature of the canopies so far, but speculative and complementary evidence for the existence of coverings over temple structures are not insubstantial.

4.5

There is no doubt that for the people of Gobekli Tepe, pillars of the sanctuaries were charged and imbued with symbolic meaning and mythological importance. Pillars are generally decorated with one or two reliefs of animals, and in some cases several patterns and motifs of various beings. It is evident that these illustrations are delivering messages and stories that hunter gatherers of Gobekli Tepe wanted the people of their own time and those to come, to know and to hear about. Long before the invention of writing - at around 3,000 BCE - the mysterious carvings of pillars presented in unison, displayed a panoramic view of the world as perceived by the hunter-gatherers of the

4.6

Golden Triangle. A world filled with fear, hope, excitement and anticipation of what the future unfolds. Scorpions and vultures, snakes and wild boars were carved into the limestones, prognostic of the mindset of the hunter-gatherers creating them - manifestations of their spirit of adventure, their dreams and ultimately their determination in challenging the forces of nature. This was the age of foraging, hunting and collecting for food and the world appeared to be an untamed, wild and uncontrollable realm.

Stories told by the reliefs of Gobekli Tepe are often eerie and hostile. One of the pillars at Enclosure C, illustrates an animated human figure with a severed head. A vulture standing over the scene is seen next to an approaching scorpion in sight. The two

Figure 104. Deep cut marks are pointed atop the head segments of Enclosure C's pillars. Four of the pillars around the periphery in this photograph show familiar incision marks which might have been used as secure footings for enclosure's rooftop beams. Archaeologists have not yet been able to discover cultural remains indicative of a roofing that would have supported a cover over the enclosure in antiquity.

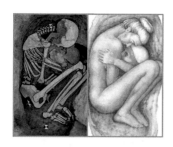

Figure 105. Artist reconstruction of a burial pit at Neolithic Catalhoyuk (right) compared against the unearthed cultural remain itself (left). The deceased is interred in fetal position, holding firm to a human crania which had already been plastered and decorated with red ochre and shell-beads, resembleing the ancestor.

Figure 106. Megalithic structures arranged in circular forms are often described as Cromlech. This one in Wiltshire, British Isles are at least 5,000 years old. One distinctive feature of Gobekli Tepe's temple pillars that does not appear in any other structure of the kind across the world is the form of the T-shaped pillars, which are made out of a single large limestone. In circular structures similar discovered elsewhere, out of the peripheries of the Near East, circular enclosures are supported by pillars that are constructed of two pieces, a shaft and a head segment.

are observing the gruesome show - a visual demonstration of numerous close at hand encounters of the people of Gobekli Tepe with the wild nature. The scene, strange as it seems, may serve as a testament to the prevalence of a well-known regional Pre-Pottery Neolithic tradition of burial across the Near East. Various sites from the central and southern Anatolian Plateau, and settlements of the Levantine corridor, display cultural remains indicative of a tradition better known as veneration of ancestors. Demonstrably, the paintings of vultures dancing and feasting over headless corpses are among the most renowned features of the Neolithic community of Catalhuyuk. In many archaeological sites across the area such as Jericho and Mureybet, the practice of veneration of ancestors was a popular mode of belief, according to which the deceased skulls were detached, preserved and passed down for generations, plastered to the likes of the ancestor, to revere their power and influence and keep their memories alive. Now let us focus on geographical prevalence of Gobekli Tepe's temple structures.

4.7

In Gobekli Tepe, the simple installations of Nevali Cori are seen in a monumental scale. The pillars are larger, taller and much more detailed with carvings and decorations unprecedented in PPN period settlements of the region. The similarity and proximity of the two sites - Nevali Cori is located less than 45 kilometers to the northwest of Gobekli Tepe - seem to be highlighting a shared reality concerned with their purpose and placement in history, that they both belonged to a network of sites and settlements flourishing in and around the 10th and 9th millennia BCE. Although the T-shaped pillars of Nevali Cori are the closest ones in characteristics and features to those of Gobekli Tepe, the presence of large metamorphic pillars in rectangular patterns have been attested in multiple PPN and Neolithic settlements of the interior of the Golden Triangle. Almost all of these settlements postdate the initial building project of Gobekli Tepe and are placed chronologically, closer to the late PPNB period. The list of settlements and sites in the

4.8

Figure 107. Pillar 43 of Enclosure D has one of the highest numbers of reliefs engraved on a single pillar. Near the bottom and adjacent to the lowermost segment of the pillar, the relief of a headless human is seen alongside a larger relief of a vulture. The two are followed immediately by a predator, a snake and a scorpion. The human head re-appears over the head segment, again held by another vulture.

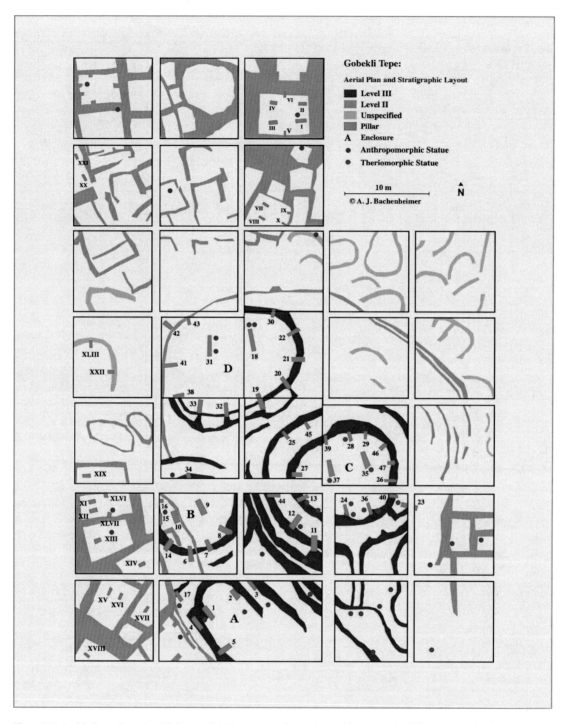

Figure 108. Aerial plan and stratigraphic layout of the Southwestern Depression and its sanctuaries. Pillars unearthed so far have been singled out by green. Structures belonging to the lowermost stratigraphic composition of the site, Level III are shown in brown, followed by the PPNB remains of Level II coloured in grey. Enclsoures A, B, C and D are further labelled.

vicinity of Gobekli hill consists of Sefer Tepe, Karahan Tepe, Urfa Yeni-Yol, Hamzan Tepe, Ayanlar Hoyuk, Harbetsuvan Tepesi, Kilisik Tepe, Gusir Hoyuk and Tasli Tepe. With shared physical features engraved on limestone T-shaped pillars, all these monolithic statues nevertheless stand in contrast, in one particular quality to the anthropomorphic creatures of Gobekli Tepe. The sanctuaries in which all these pillars are installed, are not in an oval or circular shape, but in rectangular form - and evident arrangement that is only observed in Level II temple buildings of Gobekli Tepe dating to PPNB period. A question is ought to be asked, is there a communal building concurrent to the circular temple-structures of Gobekli Tepe that follows an oval shaped pattern of architecture?

In the long list of PPN sites containing communal spaces, Jerf el-Ahmar is one that challenges certain features of Gobekli Tepe's architectural precedence. Alongside the shorelines of Euphrates and 96 kilometers to the southwest of Sanliurfa, the PPN site contains communal structures interpreted as sanctuaries, that appear in circular patterns - highly likely to belong to the PPNA period. These structures incorporate a set of domestic spaces inside, all appearing in a contiguous arrangement to the interior of the circular building, a complex fit of architecture and symbolic meaning, not yet observed at Gobekli Tepe. Semi-subterranean and fully subterranean structures of Jerf el-Ahmar are walled with cobbles analogous to the boundaries of temple sites at Gobekli Tepe but they are not supported by large T-shaped limestone pillars. In addition, the intermixture of domestic and communal spaces or better be put - the profane and the sacred - presented at Jerf el-Ahmar is challenging to the notion that at the time of Gobekli Tepe, temples had to be kept away from the residential purposed structures. The hypothesis that Gobekli Tepe was constructed by the people who knew nothing of a sedentary mode of life is now being challenged and further defied by the concession of excavators that some people such as specialists and builders might have lived at the site. It is

4.9

Figure 109. T-shaped pillars around the periphery of Nevali Cori's temple sanctuary. As one of the pillars is dug deep into the flooring of the enclosure, the other is positioned atop the benches that ran around the interior wall.

Figure 110. T-shaped pillars of the Neolithic Karahan Tepe, 35 kilometers to the southeast of Gobekli hill. Located to the east of the Harran Plain, Karahan Tepe was part of a complex set of settlements embracing cultural practices of temple construction which had originated in PPN Gobekli Tepe.

Figure 111. Frontal shaft of a T-shaped pillar from Neolithic Harbetsuvan in southern Turkey with fingers engraved synonymous to the reliefs of central pillars at Gobekli Tepe and Nevali Cori. Pillars of the Herbatsuvan are comparatively smaller then their older counterparts.

Figure 112. The communal structure at Jerf el-Ahmar on the Eurphrates river. The structure appears to have served both domestic and social purposes. It is a subterranean building of PPNA period, with a circular layout, distinctively symmetrical, that contains a central cell in the interior. Around the periphery, four separate rooms could be seen complemeneted with another much smaller space in the middle that contained a porthole near its lower base. The spaces were utilised as storage facilities where excess wild crops were kept preserved. Near the time of its abandonment, a headless corpse was laid out in the centre faced down. Archaeologists were able to recover a limestone head later under the base of a broken post that kept the structure in place.

now considered likely that there was a contemporary settlement at Gobekli Tepe.

Back to the analysis of the T-shaped pillars, a unique piece of evidence distinguishes Gobekli Tepe's anthropomorphic carvings from those of the Nevali Cori and Cayonu. At Gobekli Tepe, central pillars in some cases are adorned with single pieces of garment in shape of a loincloth that is shown to be fastened around the mid-section of the human-like pillars by the means of a thick decorated belt. Reliefs of these hide cloths are meticulously chiselled on the frontal segment of the shafts and are particularly distinctive and peculiar. In no other structure across the Neolithic or PPN Near East, pillars were featured with frontal covering high reliefs of animal hides concealing abdomen, genitals and upper thighs. This representation closely imitates impressive and distinguished physical appearance of a hunter-gatherer. The peculiarity, leaves us in a state of uncertainty, whether the people of Gobekli Tepe were hunter-gatherers or were they familiar with domestic modes of living and architecture? Contrary to the conclusions drawn by analysis of remains from Jerf el-Ahmar, the presence of animal hides carved over the pillars, could be a testimony to the nature of Gobekli Tepe's age, the modus operandi of its people and its placement in history. Whatever the underlying attribute of the messages contained in the reliefs be, the central pillars of Gobekli Tepe are imbued with such life-like human characteristics, that they leave no doubt about their anthropomorphic nature. These were meant to represent the likes of a human being. Always displayed as faceless, a feature that Schmidt believed "conveys the notion that these metamorphic creatures were not from the realm of the living men", the pillars of Gobekli Tepe have remained a mysterious and thought-provoking source of wonder at the site.

Figure 113. A younger communal building of PPN period at Jerf el-Ahmar. The structure was built to the south of the sttlement and it was fully subterranean. The circular building was supported by organic posts that were dug deep around the interior of the periphery of the bench level. Two broken pieces of base pillars have also been discovered near the benches. The enclosing wall is constructed of dry limestone rocks with no mortars used for adhesion.

Monolithic structures appear in later periods of the Neolithic Near East in abundance. These are believed to have been built as part of a renowned regional culture that came into place, following the abandonment of Gobekli Tepe and dispersal of its people throughout the region. A culture that was in addition, not only proliferated across the Near East, but might have also disseminated in the course of the following millennia across the globe. Schmidt had carefully elaborated on this notion that "in the coming millennia, various structures across the world appear to the likeness of those at Gobekli Tepe". Similarities may not necessarily indicate a correlation but we know for the fact, that collective understanding of the people of Gobekli Tepe, could have been potentially carried with the farmers of the region - descendants to the people of Gobekli Tepe - in all directions, spreading across the path of the proliferation of practices associated with agriculture and taming wild animals. In Atlit Yam, Cromlech, Barnenez, Nabta Playa, Malta, Carnac, Stonehenge and Arkaim, stone circles charged with transcendent meanings were constructed in the course of time, that appear

Figure 114. Example of a T-shaped pillar, two and a half meters tall from the PPN site of Sefer Tepe, 58 kilometers to the east of Gobekli Tepe. Sefer Tepe is located near the heart of the Golden Triangle, among a constellation of sites comprised of 11 Pre-Pottery Neolithic mounds to the south of the Taurus mountains in modern day Turkey.

Figure 115. Gobekli Tepe's Enclosure A, view from northeast. The structure has a semi-rectangular layout with the northern end haveing a half circle plan and the southern end containing a flat rectilinear wall. Five of the enclosure's pillars have been unearthed.

strikingly similar to the well-formed sanctuaries of Gobekli Tepe. Were they all parts of the same tradition? What was the underlying cause for such a global and universal undertaking? How traditions and practices associated with sanctuaries of Gobekli Tepe were manifested across the world over such a prolonged and extended period of time in history? No scientific explanation has been able to describe the connection of these phenomena to the very similar structures of the Near East. Schmidt himself was eager to keep the horizon of his hypothesis as limited as possible, confined to the Near Eastern theatre of pre-historic times, where he believed the people of Gobekli Tepe were capable of establishing intra-regional connection with and were knowing to travel to. It is noteworthy to notice that in many cases, the T-shaped pillars of analogous sites, were constructed using two separate stone slabs. A shaft and a top rock that represented the head. To the contrary, at Gobekli Tepe, all the pillars excavated are always made of one monolithic limestone. This is a particularly idiosyncratic characteristic of Gobekli's pillars that is not to be easily overlooked.

4.11

## The Central Pillars

The most typical aspect of Gobekli Tepe's sanctuaries are the pair of T-shaped pillars installed in the centre of all enclosures. At Enclosure A, these pillars are put in place in a southeasterly orientation, facing the broader landscape of Harran and the Upper Mesopotamian plain. Incidinetally, the two peripheral pillars complementing the pair are set in parallel lines to the two, establishing an arrangement of pillars appearing in a row. Pillar 5 excavated in archaeological efforts of 1996 although, is found leaning towards the northeast, perpendicular to the prevalent formation across the sanctuary and it is speculated that it would have been accompanied to the northeast by another identical pillar of the sort facing the southwesterly direction. The central pillars of enclosure, pillars 1 and 2 are left faceless, with no carvings indicative of arms or fingers on the shaft, although one bears carving of a ram engraved beneath a net of snakes and the other shows a set of reliefs with a crane, a predator and a bull in a bundle. No other pillars have been excavated in the boundaries of this sanctuary. The schematic plan of this enclosure demonstrates a semi-rectangular space, bordered in the north by a hindering crescent shaped wall. The flooring of enclosure is made of workable earth material intermixed with compound cobbles of limestone.

Enclosure B contains a set of central pillars retained in their original position at the heart of the sanctuary. The two are both decorated each with mirroring reliefs of a predator on their side profile that appears to be resembling the physical features of a fox or of a hyena. Seven peripheral pillars have been unearthed in excavations of this sanctuary, all apart one having their faces turned towards the central pair of monoliths positioned in the centre. The two central pillars of Enclosure B are too looking out to the direction of the southeast. Pillar 15 is the single lone monolith to the west of this structure that is positioned parallel to the pair of central beings. It is shorter, and it contains a large

4.12

4.13

Figure 116. Magalithic stone circles of Xaghra in Malta. One particular feature of Gobekli Tepe's T-shaped pillars is often lacking in comparisons made with the other mgalithic structures throughout the world. Gobekli Tepe's pillars are always made of one core of a limestone rock, while in other cases, the head segments are often made of a separate slab of limeston, such as this one.

Figure 117. One of the two main pillars of Enclosure D held in situ using mechanical methods. The pillar is about 5.5 meters high and is positioned on a limestone base with a depression in the centre that assisted the large pillar to saty in place. All enclosures have a pair of central pillars in the middle, all decorated with reliefs of foxes.

Figure 118. A T-shaped pillar yet attached to the rock-base it was meant to be qaurried off. The pillar is about 7 meters tall, the largest ever witnessed over the hill. It is plausible, that the project was abandoned due to the weight and enormity of the pillar which made its management almost impossible. A pillar of this size would have weighted about 60 tonnes.

Figure 119. The limestone statue of a human head was found near the southeastern corner of the western central pillar at Enclosure D. The limestone statues of this kind have been discovered in the context of most enclosures. Some are illustrated in figure 156.

cavity over the head segment, an intriguing peculiarity.

The central pillars across Gobekli Tepe have been preserved with various levels of retention and destruction over time. Some have been perfectly preserved through the course of abandonment in antiquity, whilst in instances such as Enclosure C, both pillars in the centre are broken in half and partially disposed in the course of filling the enclosure with rubbles. Laser scanning and three dimensional analysis of the rubbles can be of assistance in recreation of the original size and shape of these central pillars. Studies pertaining to analysis of these fragments are ongoing. In contrast, the pillars surrounding Enclosure C are slightly better preserved, as dismantlers have filled the gaps in between the two rounds of walls circumventing the enclosure. Schmidt as the leading excavator of the site was conscious of the operation of large machineries near the enclosures, and then proceeded to the filling of the main space. For this, archaeologists have re-erected, positioned back, and held in situ these peripheral pillars unscathed, using the same traditional methods employed thousands of years ago in the course of construction. The only surviving motif of the central pillars across this enclosure is the relief of a fox-shaped predator, decorating the eastern side of pillar 37, facing the north.

4.14

The central pillars of Enclosure C are positioned over two pedestals that are carved out of the natural limestone bedrock. The flooring surface of enclosures is also made of the original underlying core of the rock, artificially and carefully smoothened to give a flat look in antiquity. A loam cover is applied over the solid surface of the ground. The delicate flooring is then over-layered with a blanket of cobbles.

4.15

The last fully excavated enclosure of the site and the most preserved one so far, the enclosure D was discovered with the central pillars posed in an oblique position, tilted against the backfill that covers up the structure. The pair are some of the

largest and the heaviest of all pillars across the site with each applying over 30 tonnes of gross load to the bedrock beneath. The foundation at this enclosure is rather weak, compared to the previous ones and the two central pillars are held in situ on cut-out pedestals that are only 15 centimetres deep - in comparison to the Enclosure C where the pillars are kept in 35-40 centimetres depth of bedrock, the structure of this enclosure appears rather unstable and insecure. It has been suggested that the two T-shaped pillars at the centre, in conjunction to the surrounding peripheral pillars were parts of an edifice that was held in place by timber beams and a roof shelter. No material evidence in support of this theory has been unearthed so far, and it raises the question of why and how the stability of structure had been provided in antiquity.

One of the fascinating features of the central pillars of Enclosure D, is the detailed reliefs decorating the large limestone blocks.

Figure 120. Enclosure B, view from north. The two central pillars of enclosure near the lower half of the photograph are much larger and more decorated than the rest of pillars around the periphery. The enclosure has a circular layout with benches runing alongside the interior of the surrounding wall. The large porthole was discovered in-situ, somewhat between the two central pillars.

Figure 121. Enclosure C, view from northeast. The structure has a circular layout and the highest number of pillars yet discovered across the site. One of the two central pillars is broken from near the base as the other one is in half the original size. The structure had two rings of surrounding walls with a corridor in between that provided passage through the two. Some of the pillars of enclosure C are the most elaborated and the most intricate with respect to their reliefs.

The faceless, T-shaped and anthropomorphic creatures are portrayed wearing belts, bearing arms forward, covered by a fox skin loincloth, protecting their frontal parts. The belt is ornate with symbols and the fingers over the waist are clearly visible. Archaeologists working at the site had been expecting the discovery of such human-like figures for long, as pillars previously unearthed at Nevali Cori, in proximity to the site had demonstrated similar stylistic features. At the bottom of the pedestal, reliefs of birds are carved out, pacing from east towards west. The eastern central pillar contains more decorations on its belt than the western one. The western pillar on the other hand, has reliefs of a bucranium pendant wrapped around its neck, where the relief over the eastern one is rather indiscernible. These T-shaped pillars are sophisticatedly individualised, with motifs of different forms and meanings.

4.17

The sex of these central pillars is not evidently demonstrated, but by comparison to the excavated figurines from other archaeological sites of the region, Schmidt had postulated that "we are fairly certain that wearing belt has always been a characteristic of a male hunter gatherer". Nevertheless, we do not yet know if gender had played a significant role in the life of the people of Gobekli Tepe. The graffiti of a female on temple pillars of enclosure H is an example denoting the sex of a female entity at the site.

4.18

In the next pages, a summary of the pillars discovered to date is provided. Pillars are numbered according to the order of their discovery. Trenches in which they have been excavated out of could be corroborated with the figure that contains general plan of the site and its structure. Stratigraphic layers are further provided based on the report by the German Archaeological Institute. Orientation of the pillars is furthermore presented, following a posterior to anterior direction - in essence examining to what direction the frontal head segment of the pillar is faced. The set of motifs carved out on each pillar are explored in addition, with further notes that make each pillar distinguishable to the next.

Figure 122. Central pillars of Enclosure D, view from west. The two were found fully covered by the backfill and were kept in situ laying slightly to their sides. In antiquity, these pillars were firmly positioned in their place inside an elevated base that hosted a matching cavity to the lower bottom surface of the pillars. The two central pillars of Enclosure D are the largest pillars ever discovered at Gobekli Tepe with well over 5.5 meters height.

| Pillar | Trench | Enclosure | Layer | Direction | Motif | Notes |
|---|---|---|---|---|---|---|
| 1 | L9-65 | A | III | 50.5° West of North | Head-pillar left blank. Western shaft profile depicts a net of snakes over a ram. Frontal contains a set of 5 snakes, 4 approaching from the top, one is approaching from the bottom. | |
| 2 | L9-65 | A | III | 49.4° West of North | Headpillar is blank. Eastern shaft profile contains three motifs, a bull, a predator and a crane. Posterior body contains the relief of a predator. | Headpillar is damaged in both anterior and posterior sections. |
| 3 | L9-75 | A | III | 51.7° West of North | Heavily damaged. No motifs. | Abrasion and damage on either profiles and the headpillar. |
| 4 | L9-65 | A | III | 22.3° West of North | Headpillar left blank. The rest is not exacavted. | Profiles are not excavated. |
| 5 | L9-65 | A | III | 44.6° East of North | Headpillar left blank. Anterior front at the top contains relief of a snake. | |
| 6 | L9-66 | B | III | 12.9° West of North | Anterior of the headpillar contains relief of a predator. Anterior of the shaft includes relief of a snake at the top. Posterior of the shaft is blank. Side profiles of the headpillar are left blank.The excavated segments of the shaft are blank. | |
| 7 | L9-66 | B | III | 18.6° West of North | No motifs. | |
| 8 | L9-66 | B | III | 69.9° West of North | Semi-excavated. No motifs. | |
| 9 | L9-66 | B | III | 15.0° West of North | Headpillar is blank. Eastern profile of the shaft has no motifs although it contains a very small cavity near the top. Anterior segments of headpillar and the shaft are left blank. The western profile contains relief of a predator, perhaps a fox near the top. | |
| 10 | L9-66 | B | III | 22.3° West of North | Headpillar is left blank although it includes a small hole close to the middle. The frontal segments are blank. The eastern profile of the shaft contains relief of a predator, perhaps a fox mirroring the relief of Pillar 9. | The rearmost top section of the headpillar contains a cut that runs across the shorter length. |
| 11 | L9-76 | C | III | 6.8° East of North | No motifs. | Semi-excavated with the headpillar badly damaged. |

| No. | Designation | | Level | Angle | Motifs | Condition |
|---|---|---|---|---|---|---|
| 12 | L9-76 | C | III | 45.9° East of North | Eastern profile of the headpillar contains reliefs of 5 ducks. The background is depicted like a net. A relatively noticable cavity is on the lower front end of the headpillars eastern profile, immediately atop the shaft. The frontal segment of the headpillar and its western profile are left blank. The eastern segment of the shaft contains reliefs of a male predator (boar) across the top, followed by relief of a predator (fox) at the bottom. The western profile of the shaft is blank. | The inferior section of the shaft is not yet fully excavated. |
| 13 | L9-76 | C | III | 61.4° East of North | No motifs. | The pillar comes short of the enclosure's flooring. The bottom section of the shaft terminates near the height of the benches surrounding the ring. |
| 14 | L9-66 | B | III | 33.9° East of North | No motifs. | The headpillar is separated from the body and is badly damaged. The shaft is remained intact. |
| 15 | L9-66 | B | III | 7.0° West of North | No motifs. The eastern profile of the headpillar contains a relatively large hole in the middle. | The pillar is considerably shorter in size relative to the rest. |
| 16 | L9-66 | B | III | 62.7° West of North | No motifs. | The headpillar and the shaft are badly damaged. |
| 17 | L9-65 | A or Bordering Enclosure of L9-55 | III | 38.9° West of North | The upper segment of the headpillar is exposed with no motifs visible. | The pillar is not yet excavated. |
| 18 | L9-78 | D | III | 9.8° West of North | Headpillar contains no motifs. The western profile of the shaft includes the relief of a bent arm that begins from the upper frontal portion of the shaft and runs diagonal to the height of the pillar in a < shape reaching the posterior mid-section of the shaft (the elbow), making a sharp angle of 54° symmetrical to the upper half, terminating at the lower frontal facade of the shaft with 5 pointed fingers in a tight order. Near the frontal portion of the elbow, the relief of a predator (a fox) is carved, synonymcus to those of | Pillar 18 stands 5.5 meters tall, one of the largest pillars at the complex. It is losely positioned over the base that contains a large depression in the middle filled with gravel, creating a desirable sitting space for the pillar. The rear western end of the headpillar in the middle |

| # | | | | | |
|---|---|---|---|---|---|
| | | | | the central pillars of enclosures B and C. The eastern profile of the shaft includes the same pattern of arms and elbow, in exclusion of the relief of the predator. The middle section of the shaft on either profile contains a narrow strip perpendicular to the height of the pillar (a belt). The strip includes figures CCHCHⵔ. To the front, the shaft shows relief of a predator's hide with long tail (a fox) and both arms hanging from the middle section of the strip (belt) covering the mid and the lower segments of the shaft. The belt buckle on the western side includes patterns of I, H and H respectively from the top to the bottom and across the eastern edge, patterns of I and I positioned right across one another. The eastern profile of the shaft includes the same strip continued, albeit with a brief pattern of CHⵔ. The upper frontal segment of the shaft includes relief of a V shaped strip necklace with a pendant composed of patterns H at the top and O at the bottom. The southern segment of pillar 18 base slab consists of reliefs of 7 ducks moving towards west. | contains a narrow depression before the terminating edge. |
| 19 | L9-78 | D | 18.7° West of North | The relief of a snake is carved on the lower portion of the headpillar's frontal segment, moving towards the floor. | The shaft is trapped on all sides to a considerable height by a sequence of mid-sized flat stones. |
| 20 | L9-78 | D | 42.2° West of North | No motifs on the headpillar. The side profiles of the shaft are left blank. The frontal segment of the shaft contains reliefs of a snake at the top, a bull in the middle and a predator (a fox) at the bottom. | Semi-excavated. The shaft is trapped in the surrounding sequence of flat stone slabs. |
| 21 | L9-78 | D | 78.6° West of North | No motifs on the headpillar. The southern profile of the shaft contains reliefs of two games, one carved atop the other. The relief over the top appears to have sharp pointed horns while the one in the bottom is synonymous in shape to the relief of a ram from pillar 1. | |
| 22 | L9-78 | D | 71.4° East of North | No motifs on the headpillar. The southern profile of the shaft includes relief of a predator (a fox). The frontal segment of the shaft albeit contains relief of a snake in the upper middle section moving towards the ground. | |

106

| No. | Code | C | III | Angle | Description | Notes |
|---|---|---|---|---|---|---|
| 23 | L9-86 | C | III | 73.0° West of North | Northern profile of the headpillar contains descending reliefs of three ducks. The rest of the pillar is left blank. | The western termination of the surface above the headpillar includes a deep cut parallel to the length of the headpillar. |
| 24 | L9-86 | C | III | 14.8° West of North | No reliefs. | The headpillar is badly damaged. |
| 25 | L9-77 | C | III | 45.4° West of North | No reliefs. | This is a much smaller pillar positioned at the outer edge of the second ring surrounding Enclosure C. |
| 26 | L9-87 | C | III | 82.1° West of North | Side profiles of the headpillar contain no motifs. The frontal segment of the headpillar has a relief of a predator (possibly a boar) in its mid-section. The shaft's side profiles and the frontal piece contain no motifs. | The rear southern end of the headpillar terminates in a downward angle with a depression cut that runs parallel to the length of the headpillar. |
| 27 | L9-77 | C | III | 88.9° West of North | The headpillar contains no motifs. The side profiles of the shaft are left blank. The frontal segment of the shaft at the top includes a 3 dimensional relief of a predator that stands out distinguishably out of the hosting rock. The predator is facing downwards in direction of the enclosure's floor. Beneath the large sculpture, a 2 dimensional relief of another predator is carved, a wild boar, facing north. | The frontal western termination of the headpillar contains a deep depression cut. |
| 28 | L9-87 | C | III | 17.3° West of North | The anterior section of the headpillar contains relief of a boar at the top. Western profile of the shaft has a relief of another large boar near the top, adjacent to the enclosure's interior walls and mid-way through the headpillar. The frontal segment of the shaft includes relief of a pendant over the top shaped in form of a θ. The lower section of the shaft contains rel ef of a belt buckle, in form of a capital l or a cpital H sideways. | The above portion of the frontal southern termination of headpillar contains a deep depression cut. |
| 29 | L9-87 | C | III | 10.9° East of North | Headpillar contains no motifs. Side profiles of the shaft are left blank. The frontal segment of :he shaft contains relief of a belt buckle over the bottom, in shape of a H. Right beneath the belt buckle, relief of a boar is carved. | |

| # | ID | | | Orientation | Description | Notes |
|---|---|---|---|---|---|---|
| 30 | L9-78 | D | III | 19.8° East of North | Either profiles contain no motifs. The frontal segment of the headpillar includes relief of a capital I or H sideways over the top. The lower eastern segment of the headpillars frontal piece, contains relief of a snake heading downwards in direction of the floor. The western segment of the lower headpillar's anterior is left blank. The upper frontal segment of the shaft, immediately below the headpillar contains 5 sets of reliefs, all carved right next to one another. The set includes, 4 snakes, two of a large size and a pair of smaller size. Towards the western edge, the relief of a ◎ is carved. | The pillar is of relatively smaller height in the context of Enclosure D's enormous pillars. Profile headpillar contains a large cavity near the mid-top section. The above surface of the headpillar in entirety, contains a large depression cut that runs parallel across the headpillar's length. |
| 31 | L9-68 | D | III | 15.3° West of North | Headpillar is left blank. The western profile of the shaft includes relief of a bent arm that begins from the upper frontal portion of the shaft and runs diagonal to the height of the pillar in a < shape reaching the posterior mid-section of the shaft (the elbow), making a sharp angle symmetrical to the upper half, terminating at the lower frontal facade of the shaft with 5 pointed fingers in a tight order. The eastern profile of the shaft includes the same pattern of arms and elbow. The middle section of the shaft on either profile contains a narrow strip perpendicular to the pillars height (possibly a belt) that contains no reliefs. The frontal segment of the shaft includes relief of a predator's hide with long tail (a fox) and both arms hanging from either sides. The upper segment of the frontal shaft contains relief of a pendant in form of a bucranium with horns turned towards the floor. The base of this pillar has no motifs. | This pillar is one of the largest at the Gobekli complex alongside pillar 18. In comparison to the said pillar, it contains simpler motifs and less complexity. The pillar is positioned on the base slab in a similar fashion to pillar 18. |
| 32 | L9-67 | D | III | 9.3° West of North | No reliefs. | |
| 33 | L9-67 | D | III | 14.7° East of North | Western profile of the headpillar contains no motifs. The eastern profile of the headpillar, closer to the front shows a set of 3 ducks (geese) in descending order. The frontal segment of the headpillar has no reliefs. Eastern profile of the shaft contains reliefs of two large cranes near (or in) | This pillar contains one of the highest numbers of motifs. The above surface of the headpillar, the northern termination has a depression cut in the middle |

| 34 | L9-67 | B | III | 20.9° West of North | the water (or appearing above a sequence of swerving snakes). The western profile of the shaft has a relief of a predator adjacent to the enclosure's interior wall. Over the lower section, the profile shows rows of snakes, but their heads appears to surface across the frontal sheft's western edge. The frontal portion of the shaft contains a set of complex reliefs. On its eastern side, a narrow strip of symbols run down alongside the edge. Over the top, there are 26 capital Lambda shaped figures Λ one above the other, all the way to the mid-section. These might simply represent the continuation of the water waves or snakes (or both) that appeared on the eastern profile. From the mid-point onwards all the way to the floor's direction, the symbols take the shape of thick round-cornered triangles ▷ analogous to regular snake heads across the site. On the opposite side, along the edge, the strip contains Lambda shaped figures at the top all the way to the mid-section of the shaft that is followed by a series of H shaped symbols towards the bottom. Closer to the bottom of the shaft and on the western edge, snake heads appear again, symmetrical to the figures of the eastern strip. In between the tow rows of symbols, and in the central facade of the frontal shaft, a range of figures have been carved from top to the bottom. Multiple small-sized cranes at the top are followed beneath by a set of three snakes side-by-side headed towards the floor. In the middle of the facade the relief of a large H shaped symbol is carved. A seven-legged scorpion (spider) underneath faces the H shaped symbol. Towards the bottom of the frontal shaft, another series of three snakes are carved moving towards the floor. The three are countered by another eight-legged scorpion (spider) that appears to be crawling out from underneath the pillar. | that runs alongside the length of the surface. |
| | | | | No motifs. | | Not fully excavated. This is a relatively short and small pillar positioned on the outer edge of Enclosure B. |

| # | ID | | | Orientation | Motifs | Condition |
|---|---|---|---|---|---|---|
| 35 | L9-87 | C | III | 17.1° West of North | No motifs. | Badly damaged. The pillar contains no head portion and the shaft is broken in half. |
| 36 | L9-86 | C | III | 23.9° West of North | No motifs. | Badly damaged. The headpillar is broken into multiple pieces. A depression cut rund parallel the entire above surface of the headpillar. |
| 37 | L9-87 | C | III | 24.8° West of North | Eastern profile over the top contains relief of a predator facing south, synonymous in shape to the central pillars of enclosures B and D. Base slab has no motifs. | Damaged. The headpillar and the upper segment of of the shaft are missing. The remaining shaft is broken into two pieces. The pillar is positioned over, inside the base's depression. The depression is subsequently filled with concrete like terrazzo. |
| 38 | L9-68 | D | III | 64.3° East of North | Northern profile contains no motifs. The southern shaft contains relief of a predator near the top (possibly a fox) and a wild boar in the middle. The reliefs are followed towards the bottom of the shaft by a set of three cranes moving towards east. The frontal segment of the shaft contains relief of an Omega shaped Ω pendant near the top and two plain strips on either sides of the facade. | Southern surface of the headpillar contains a cavity hole near bottom frontal section of the piece. |
| 39 | L9-77 | C | III | 16.6° West of North | No motifs. | The headpillar has a plain rectangular shaped depression near its southwestern corner. |
| 40 | L9-86 | C | III | 65.2° West of North | The mid-section of the frontal shaft includes reliefs of 5 fingers on both sides, symmetrical. The reliefs immitate the position of resting both hands over the abdomen. | The pillar's surface overall is badly abraded. |
| 41 | L9-68 | D | III | 87.5° West of North | No motifs. | Badly damaged. The headpillar is broken off the shaft and the pillar's surface abraded all over. |

| No. | ID | Type | Tier | Orientation | Motifs | Notes |
|---|---|---|---|---|---|---|
| 42 | L9-68 | D | | 46.6° West of North | Headpillar contains no motifs. The frontal shaft contains relief of a snake at the top moving towards the floor. Immediately beneath, the relief of a duck is carved | Semi-excavated. The lower shaft is not yet exposed. |
| 43 | L9-68 | D | III | 21.1° West of North | Headpillar's western surface contains a complex set of reliefs. Three geese (or baskets) are shown side-by-side, in between which appear reliefs of a predator, a boar and a crane. Underneath the upper section, a series of patterns appear in wave-like forms of V and Λ in the middle. To the south the swerving patterns are sided by reliefs of a crane, a snake that is moving towards the floor and two symbols of H and H sideways. To the opposit end of the shaft and near the northern edge, adjacent to the enclosure's wall, the relief of a vulture is carved with a V shaped sign below the neck. The vulture is in a seated position, holding a circular (spherical) shape in the left (southern) hand (wing). The reliefs are separated by a horizontal line, levelled with the divorcing line that sets apart the headpillar from the shaft. Over the western shaft, a large eight-legged scorpion is carved moving upwards. Near the northern wall of the enclosure, the shaft contains reliefs of a snake over the top, next to the scorpion's head. Beneath is carved the relief of a predator (possibly a boar) followed by another snake smaller in size. Over the bottom, the relief of a vulture (or a bird) is shown, right next to the relief of what appears to be a headless human figure with erect penis. The frontal segment of the headpillar shows relief of a predator in 2 dimesnional form moving downwards, encountering relief of a scorpion. Two narrow plain strips run along the length of the shaft's front. | The head section of this pillar is exceptionally large, possibly for the purpose of hosting the complex set of reliefs. The southern corner of the shaft's western profile, near the relief of the headless being is broken and worn away, rendering the analysis of the scene more difficult. |
| 44 | L9-76 | C | III | 84.9° East of North | No motifs. | One of the smaller sized pillars of Enclosure C exterior edge. Semi-excavated. |
| 45 | L9-77 | C | III | 22.9° West of North | No motifs. | One of the smaller sized pillars of the outer edge of Enclosure C. Not yet exposed. |

| 46 | L9-87 | C | III | 71.5° East of North | No motifs. | Badly damaged. The headpillar is grossly abraded and the shaft is broken near the base. |
| 47 | L9-87 | C | III | In-situ 81.6° East of North | No reliefs. | Dislocated. The pillar is currently positioned leaning against the interior bench-walls of the Enclosure C across surface. This is a much smaller sized pillar with a narrow width. |

Figure 124. Pillars 1, 2, 3 and 5 (left to right) from Enclosure A.

Figure 125. Pillars 6, 7, 8 and 9 of Enclosure B (from left to right).

Figure 126. Pillars 10, 11, 12 and 13 (from left to right) repsectively from enclosures B, C, C, C.

Figure 127. Pillars 14, 15, 16 and 17 (from left to right) of Enclosures B, B, B and either A/B.

Figure 128. Pillars 18, 19, 20 and 21 (from left to right) all of Enclosure D.

Figure 129. Pillars 22, 23, 24 and 26 (from left to right) of Enclosures D, C, C, C.

114

Figure 130. Pillars 27, 28, 29 and 30 (from left to right) respectively of Enclosures C, C, C, D.

Figure 131. Pillars 32, 33, 33 (another view) and 35 (from left to right) of Enclosures D, D and C.

Figure 132. Pillars 38, 39, 40 and 42 (from left to right) of Enclosures D, C, C, D.

Figure 133. Pillars 43, 45, 46 and 47 (from left to right) respectively of Enclosures D, C, C, C.

# 5

## CHAPTER FIVE

### COMPLEMENTARY FEATURES OF THE SITE

## The Portholes

Another set of important architectural features which are presented in many enclosures at Gobekli Tepe are monolithic stones that are shaped in form of rocky basins with central holes in the middle and have been discovered in various locations across the site. From a stratigraphic point of view, none of these have been uncovered near the surface and they are all unearthed during the course of clearing out backfill from within lower strata of almost all enclosures. Preliminary studies suggested that these could have been utilised as window frames or porthole stones providing access to the structures present at the site. Although these stone frames were unearthed in situ and often at the bottom of enclosures' filling debris and sediments, the possibility is that they were in fact originally in vertical positions, facilitating entry in and out of enclosures for the purpose of controlling access to the sanctuaries.

The deduction has been recently challenged following propositions on the placement of one of these portholes at Enclosure B. The portal stone was found laid in the centre of the inner space - in a proximal location separating the two central pillars of the building, slightly further to the south. It has been lately postulated that the porthole's current location might be prognostic of its original setting, right in the centre of a possible roof-top that covered the enclosure in antiquity. Should this have been the initial placement of the porthole before the abandonment of Enclosure B, the enormous weight, size and complexity of its fitting incorporated into the covering apparatus of the sanctuary must have required outstanding technological development.

The deep sounding across the northern boundaries of Enclosure B has yielded another monolith of the kind, carved out with careful thought and intention in depth of the outer enclosing wall. The porthole is 2.1 meters wide and 2.3 meters high. It

5.1

5.2

119

Figure 134. The large limestone porthole in-situ inside Enclosure B was found somewhat between the two central pillars (to the right hand side of the photograph). The porthole's interior framing has a rectangular layout and it is speculated that it might have been positioned in anqtiquity at the centre of a rooftop that covered the enclosure. Other hypotheses, one suggested by Schmidt himself considered the porthole to have been placed vertically right at the entrance to the interior of the enclsoure.

contains an opening of 91x83 centimeters aperture, right beneath the carving of a bucranium. Two predators on both fringes of the opening safeguarded the means of entry. A perpendicular pillar positioned to the north of the eastern central pillar of Enclosure D has also provided a porthole that is much smaller and is more simple in size and shape, uncharacteristic of the enclosure's generally sophisticated metamorphic features.

One of the trenches to the Northwestern Mound of the hill revealed a double porthole, hidden deep beneath the surface. The fascinating portal, functioned as a double door entry frame in and out of an enclosure - yet undisclosed - protected by high reliefs of three predatory animals, alongside carvings of a swerving snake placed on the southern rim of the monolith. A similar porthole of this type has been previously uncovered in

5.3

the PPNA sanctuary of Jerf el-Ahmar, near the ground level of the mid-cell structure built in between the two symmetrical doorless rooms to the interior of the sanctuary. Jerf el-Ahmar's porthole is dug in the lower portion of the wall and lacks the meticulously carved out motifs of the similar types at Gobekli Tepe. A porthole stone fragment from Ayanlar Hoyuk, a PPN settlement near the vicinity of Gobekli Tepe has also been excavated. It appears that in the context of cultural traditions of the PPN Near East, construction of these architectural features was customary.

## Complementary Architectural Features

Geo-magnetic profiling and studies conducted with the use of ground penetrating radar, have made it clear that Gobekli Tepe contains various and numerous types of monolithic enclosures. These enclosures, different in size and shape are situated across large segments of the hilltop and each is unique in its architectural and stylistic features. Since 2006, structures of smaller size and different shapes have been subjected to exclusive archaeological excavations across the northwestern corner of the hill. Over the edge of the ridge, archaeological efforts have led to the discovery of fascinating finds and cultural remains. Although many of these structures do not pre-date the larger colossal buildings of the Southwestern Depression, they contain valuable information on the usage and the purpose of their construction. During the course of excavations in 2009, a semi-circular terrace wall was discovered marking the partition line of a complex of temple buildings to the southwest - including enclosures A, B, C, D, G and F - from smaller structures with simple design to the northwestern corner of the hill. The find may clearly indicate that sanctuaries at Gobekli Tepe were kept out spatially separate from the rest of structures at the site. What was the function of the remaining buildings to the northwest is the subject of speculations to this date.

5.4

5.5

Figure 135. Another porthole of a square-shaped layout was found deep beneath the outer exterior of the northwestern corner at Enclosure B.

Figure 136. A sondage to the northwestern corner of the wall surrounding Enclosure B yielded this porthole (same as figure 135). The framing contains reliefs of two predators guarding the entrance on opposite sides when over the top, an auroch's head is carved with its horns clearly distinguishable.

Figure 137. A double porthole was discovered in 2009 inside the lowermost surface of one of the trenches to the northwest of the hill. A large snake is carved over the framing as it approaches three guarding predators.

Figure 138. The stairs unearthed deep beneath the southern corridor leading way to Enclosure C from south. They are the oldest ones ever found constructed by hunter-gatherers.

Figure 139. Aerial photography of the trench L9-85 shows the set of stairs (lower bottom of the photograph) as they open to the corridor that later leads to the Enclosure C further to the north. The stairs are less than a meter wide and they progressively shrink in size as they near the corridor entrance.

Figure 140. The relief of a boar on his back is carved right at the centre of an entry to the corridor leading to the Enclosure C. The limestone containing relief of a boar comes less than a meter apart from another U shaped monolith that contained statues of two predators guarding the entry. One of the predators of the U shaped block is missing (Figure 154).

Enclosure C situated to the southern trenches of the Southwestern Depression has disclosed a particularly peculiar feat of architecture that is strikingly interesting. This is the first flight of stairs yet discovered in history. It dates back to 11,500 years ago and it is made out of a single bridge of a limestone rock that is partitioned to regular deep treads and right-angled rises and is complemented by flat stone slabs positioned over the steps. The run is about two and a half meters long and two meters high and is oriented towards the northwest, opening to an enclosed corridor of entry, distant from the outer boundary walls of Enclosure C by 8 meters. The flight of stairs is comprised of 9 set of steps, all about the same height and depth. Adjacent to the opening of the corridor, the stairs end near a U shaped portal decorated with reliefs of a wild beast that appears immediately before a larger limestone rock containing relief of a boar that is laid on its back. The iconography of these set of monoliths is immersed with intentions to communicate meaning and abstract art.

5.6

## The Backfill

Gobekli Tepe's geographical location was of a paramount importance. Sanctuaries were constructed over a large hill that was situated to the opening of the lowlands of Harran in northern Syria and the upper Mesopotamian region of the Khabur basin. The in-situ temple-structures of Gobekli Tepe could have been recognised from far distant positions miles away. It occurs to an observer, how such an astounding complex of temples could have been forgotten and could have been hidden from the memories and the eyes of the people for thousands and thousands of years? The answer lies in the way that enclosures were vacated and preserved in antiquity. When decisions were made to abandon one of the sanctuaries, the people of Gobekli Tepe filled them up with tonnes and tonnes of sediments, stone fragments, animal remains, lithic flints and debris of all kinds. The backfill material would make up even height with the maximum elevation of an enclosure, often all the way to the top. The fill would cover the entirety of a structure, before another one was constructed either over the top, or alongside its peripheries. Archaeologists have removed many thousand cubic meters of debris in the course of excavations at Gobekli Tepe. The recovered material is not sterile and it is rich with artefacts - chiefly flints, flakes, sculptures, animal bones and in some rare cases human remains, which is not quite unexpected in a site of this magnitude. Apart from the radiocarbon dating methods, archaeologists can utilise typological schemes to sort out the nature of all flint tools and arrowheads discovered through the backfill. This procedure sheds light on the age and technologies associated with the construction of enclosures. Furthermore the stone tools recovered could be juxtaposed against those obtained throughout the other concurrent settlements of the region, in the context of lithic industries found in archaeological horizons of the entire Near East, during the same time period of Gobekli Tepe's construction.

Classification of the lithic recovered is dominated by Khiamian points. These arrowheads appear in an intermediary phase of the Near Eastern archaeology, falling right after the end of the Natufian period and preceding the arrival of PPNA. Gobekli Tepe lithic furthermore are comprised of Helwan points and those of Nemrik, Byblos and Tell Aswad type-site further to the south. Tell Aswad is best known for its cache of curated skulls, plastered and decorated as part of the regional tradition of veneration of ancestors. With all the similarities at hand, one piece of evidence across Gobekli Tepe's lithic assemblage is missing. That is Nevali Cori points that appear in the rarest number throughout the site. Lithic industries of the later PPNB period are also generally absent, apart from traditions that are closely associated with the earliest centuries of the PPNB era - an indication of the abandonment of Gobekli Tepe soon after mid-PPNB period at around 8,500 BCE.

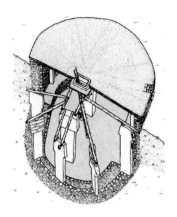

Figure 141. Artist reconstruction of a proposition that hypothesises the placement of the porthole at the centre of Encloure B, over the rooftop covering of the structure.

Figure 142. Curated and plastered human crania from PPN Tell Aswad in Syria. Similar plastered skulls have been found at Jericho and other PPN sites of the region.

Figure 143. Khiamian arrowheads are shown in the centre of a lithic assemblage from Gobekli Tepe. The group contains Helwan, Khiamian, Nemrik and Byblos points.

Figure 144. Enclosure B before the final phase of excavations, view from northwest. Dense backfill material is seen covering the entire space. The filling debris depositioned at the time of abandonment had buried the structure in its entirety.

Figure 145. Bedrock depressions carved in the limestone surface of the ridge. Some of the cistern shaped holes are dug in deep whilst cup-sized ones are often scattered around the hill. Gobekli Tepe's man-made mound could be seen in the background. Schmidt suggested that these depressions might have been created in antiquity to contain and preserve water needed by the people of Gobekli Tepe, engaged in construction of the site and quarrying the T-shaped pillars.

## Bedrock Depressions

Nearest aquifers to the Gobekli hill, capable of producing water streams close to the ground are about 5 kilometres to the south of the ridge. The reality raises the question of how monumental structures of Gobekli Tepe were constructed in antiquity when the builders of these enclosures had ought to be supplied with drinking water and sources of sustenance. In numerous places adjacent to the set of enclosures, the bedrock limestone trending in the southeasterly direction is carved deep, where cistern shaped depressions are dug in various depths and forms within the bedrock. Klaus Schmidt had suggested that these were utilised in forms of water storage systems and drainage facilities. Their purpose is albeit unknown but the German archaeologist postulated that these scattered depressions across the bedrock were purposed to reserve precipitation received across the landscape to be channelised back into the vicinity of the sanctuaries. It appears that such logistical feats were instrumental in accommodation of the labourers and construction of the site all year round, as multiple bands of hunter-gatherers present at the quarries were engaged in persistent and labourious task of producing the T-shaped pillars and constructing the surrounding structures.

5.9

## Flora and Fauna

Ritual practices and dietary habits of the people of Gobekli Tepe could be gleaned from the study of animal remains unearthed across the site. Faunal remains will furthermore present a range of ancient fauna that existed near the site and throughout the landscape at the time of Gobekli Tepe's usage. Recent research has demonstrated deposition of a wide range of faunal remains - dominated by gazelle and other taxa such as wild cattle, wild ass, foxes, wild boar, sheep and goat. There is no evidence of domesticated class of species across the site. The fact comes into support of a major hypothesis that the people of Gobekli Tepe

5.10

were hunters and gatherers who preceded the fast approaching impacts of the Neolithic lifeways - the emergence of animal husbandry and cultivation of crops. Further studies focused on archaeo-botanical elements present throughout the backfill is also underway, with preliminary finds pointing out the accounted for plants recovered across the site belonging to a distinct group of botanical species isolated genetically from the later domesticated founder crops.

Back to the question of Gobekli Tepe's animal remains, the size of the faunal assemblage at the site appears to be rather substantial and quite considerable for a mere hunter-gatherer community of that old. The number of faunal remains attested in the first phases of excavations from 1996 to 2001 exceeds an striking number of 130,000 identified specimen, indicating intensive and methodical predation of the surrounding environment to an unprecedented scale for the purposes of

5.11

Figure 146. Gazelle horn exposed in-situ through the fill. Based on the analysis of faunal material recovered, archaeologists can reconstruct the dietary intake of the people at Gobekli Tepe, what they were eating, what were their desired games and how intensively they went about chasing those in the wild. Faunal remains do tell us as well about the animals consumed themselves, if they were domesticated or wild, if the male ones were targeted more frequently than the female ones and at what age the prey is put down by their human hunters.

Figure 147. Seven ducks are carved on the southern profile of the limestone base of pillar 18, Enclosure D. The ducks are strolling towards west from east and they are carved evenly spread out across the pedestal's frontpiece. It has been suggested that the piece indicates close observation of regular seasonal movements of birds flying over the region.

Figure 148. The frontal portion of pillar 33 contains a set of complex reliefs. In between the tow rows of symbols, and in the central facade, a range of figures have been carved. Multiple small-sized cranes at the top are followed beneath by three snakes side-by-side headed towards the floor. In the middle of the facade the relief of a large H shaped symbol is carved. A seven-legged scorpion (spider) underneath faces a H shaped symbol. Towards the bottom, another set of snakes are carved moving towards the floor. The three are countered by another eight-legged scorpion (spider) that appears to be crawling out from underneath the pillar.

communal feasting and intensive ritual practices. The relatively large presence of remains associated with foxes, in comparison to the rest of the settlements across the region appears to be an atypical characteristic of Gobekli Tepe, positioning this species relatively notable in the hierarchy of the local economy.

Whether the recovered animal remains at Gobekli Tepe belong to a wild or domesticated taxa is carefully explored by cross-comparison of the finds with those of the early domesticated remains unearthed in the near regional network of sites around the periphery of the Golden Triangle, specifically those of the PPN Gurcu Tepe and the exposed assemblages of Nevali Cori. Studies are generically concentrated on the size of skeletal tissues and micro-morphological features of the remains, and whether these characteristics of the kind contend in with the widely known features of recognised domesticated taxa excavated from across sites of the Near East. Joris Peters, an specialist in analysis of animal remains of the Ludwig Maximilian University of Munich who is in charge of faunal studies at Gobekli Tepe, describes the overall characteristics of the assemblage obtained across the site and through the backfill as belonging to a diverse range of particularly wild species. The observation has been a universal feature of the site, regardless of in which layer or pit the faunal remains were deposited in antiquity and were subsequently unearthed in modern times. Identified faunal assemblage recovered from Gobekli Tepe is comprised of mainly gazelle, aurochs, Asiatic wild ass, and wild sheep. Red fox, wild boar and wild cat, each constitute a relatively small percentage of unearthed fauna, whilst gazelle and red deer notably dominate the assemblage with almost 52 per cent of mammalian finds. Aurochs comes in second with roughly 17 per cent of the total identified specimen. The dietary intake of the users of the site must have relied ostensibly to a sizeable degree on wild cattle - that is accounting for the high number of subsistence portions obtained per species in this case, relative to the other taxa.

5.12

## Desirability of the Prey

The relationship between the variety of species reflected in animal remains assemblage at the site and the reliefs, carvings and statues of animals in the sanctuaries is a curious one that is ought to be explored. Schmidt himself had extensively placed the onus of emphasis on depictions of wild predators at Gobekli Tepe, with their teeth and horns exposed and their claws obtrusive to the naked eyes. He insisted that such attempts in deliberate manifestation of the beings viciousness presented in art, relates to the wild nature of prey pursued at large in the hunting and gathering mode of life of the people of Gobekli Tepe. The crude prominence of fierce, natural faculties of the animals are described to be in correspondence symmetrically to the faunal finds extracted throughout the fill - with feral, untamed and undomesticated specimen dominating the picture.

Although the dichotomy of domesticated and wild embodies a powerful characterisation of what is manifest on the surface, complexities beneath the outer apparent edges are in multitudes. In spite of the fact that all species butchered at the site were undomesticated, the assemblage is overwhelmed by remains of wild gazelles and wild cattle, carvings of which are amongst the most infrequent reliefs appearing across the site. In contrast, reliefs of snakes, ducks and cranes depicted in high frequency site-over comprise a tacit miserable, meager proportion of the faunal remains recovered. One way to resolve this conundrum of high complication, is to perceive that reliefs of enclosures are indications of desirability of a prey, the allure of the animals hunted in small numbers and the attractiveness of scarcity. Foxes, wild boar and mouflon were amongst these. They were found to comprise an insignificant proportion of the identified species at the site, although their remains are yet present to the eyes. These scarce species, the rare ones, are the ones decorated far more frequently than the plentiful over the pillars and across enclosures, therefore describing depictions of the sort, as a form

5.13

5.14

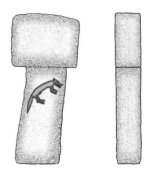

Figure 149. Author's reconstruction of Pillar 9 (eastern central pillar) of Enclosure B with relief of a male fox carved on the upper half of the side profile of the shaft. Central pillars of all enclosures apart from Enclosure A, contain reliefs of foxes engraved on their side profiles. In case of Enclosure D, it appears that within their arms, the anthroporomorphic creatures are holding foxes they have already hunted for. The two pillars are also sporting a fox hide loincloth covering their abdomen and groin areas.

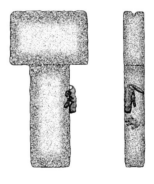

Figure 150. Author's reconstruction of pillar 27 of Enclosure C, containing a three-dimensional statue of a predator (perhaps a lion) standing out of the hosting rock. The predator approaches a wild boar that is carved out of the limestone shaft and is engraved directly beneath. There appears to be a connection between the desirability of a prey and its relative representation in reliefs of Gobekli Tepe.

Figure 150. A stone slab from Enclosure D showing a detached human head (upper centre) near relief of a predator (centre), a vulture (right), and another animal (upper left). The iconography of the scene resembles decorations of pillar 43 (Figure 107) and is reminiscent of a PPN tradition of veneration of ancestors that included collecting the deceased crania for preservation and further ritual/ceremonial practices.

of invocation, a transcendent summoning of their essence for the desire of a greater amount. This approach is also capable of describing the prevalence of reliefs known to be of snakes and bears. These were not only the rarest of species represented in the assemblage, they were amongst the wildest and the most untamed, the forces of which were ought to be captivated, controlled and commanded over.

### Mortuary Practices and the Limestone Statues

Limestone statues are ubiquitous in the context of the landfill discharged within the interior of enclosures. Remains of anthropomorphic sculptures have been found to the southwest of Enclosure A, near the western boundaries of Enclosure B and close to the central pillars of Enclosure D. Statues of animal form, on the other hand, have been unearthed at enclosures A and C in multitudes. Particularly the southern interior wall of Enclosure C contains a matrix of theriomorphic sculptures adjacent to the pillars 12, 13, 23, 24, 36 and 40. A concentration of 8 theriomorphic limestone statues in this enclave is profoundly thought provoking. A pair of monolithic vessels and theriomorphic finds precisely to the southern base of the central pillars at this enclosure is furthermore enticing to the eye. Enclosure B albeit is one that includes the lowest number of such finds across the site. One single vessel has been unearthed near the northern base of pillar 9, accompanied by an anthropomorphic sculpture to the western interior wall of the sanctuary, its placement near pillar 5 a cause of ontological interest.

The backfill supporting the central pillars of Enclosure D, contains segments of statuesque limestones positioned to the east of pillar 31 and to the southern base of pillar 18. These are deliberately placed immediately adjacent to the pillars. Unearthed from down below the backfill sediments, a limestone figure was discovered in 2010 formed and chiseled in shape of a human skull. As noted before, special treatment of skulls and their removal from the human corpus was a customary practice of the PPN period. These skulls were collected, deposited in pits, and in many occasions such as the famous finds of Jericho, were venerated and shaped with the help of clay and plaster to the likeness of the deceased features.

Various theories have been suggested to describe the finding of the human limestone heads. One of the mainly accepted propositions, argues that the head segments could have been originally a component of larger massive human shaped figures, much similar to the Urfa statue. The function of the statue might have been to protect the enclosures and sanctuaries as life-sized guards to the portholes. These statues have earthly shapes and characteristics which stand in contrast with massive faceless T-shaped pillars of the site. This proposition is also supported by

Figure 151. The statue of a wild boar was discovered in-situ near the mid section of a T-shaped pillar. As debris around the pillar were later dug out, the pillar exhibited relief of a boar on its side profile immediately next to the area where the statue was found.

Figure 152. Additional excavations around pillar 12 reveals relief of a boar and a fox, right next to the place where the statue of a boar had been earlier uncovered.

Figure 153. The limestone head unearthed near the base of a roof post at Jerf el-Ahmar. Similar limestone heads have been found at Nevali Cori, Gobekli Tepe and other communities of PPN and Neolithic of the Near East.

5.15

5.16

129

Figure 154. Schematic reconstruction of the U shaped limestone rock that was found in-situ at the entry to the corridor of Enclosure C. The lion figures on both ends guarded the U shaped passage way.

Figure 155. A totem composed of limestone, depicting multiple stories and figures, with an integrated composition. Although the face portion of the head segment is disfigured, it belongs to a wild animal. The arms are curving from the sides to meet in the front, right above the arms of another figure that are joined in the front. Under these a human figure with visible head and arms reaches forward, holding on to a libation vessel. The sides show snakes undulating upwards. (Length: 188 cm Width: 35 cm)

the reality that portholes are often protected on the sides by high reliefs of wild animals anchored against the main stone frame. In previous sections, examples of the sort were discussed. In some instances, such as enclosure C, the pillars and walls are carved out with real size figures of wild boar, leopards and carnivorous animals, showing their teeth and claws, reinforcing the hypothesis that limestone heads might belong to real life size statues. One of the most current excavation campaigns led by the late Klaus Schmidt in 2010, yielded the remains of a large and complex anthropomorphic sculpture, reminiscent of a totem pole. Schmidt had reminded me that "if such samples had existed in Neolithic times, many would have been decayed throughout the course of the following millennia, as they would have been most likely built of timber or organic material purposed to be lighter of weight and easily portable." The stone statue albeit was buried about two meters beneath the surface of a rectangular structure of Layer II and somewhat represents a complex figure with phallus, giving brith to a much smaller human high relief. Although the face is entirely destroyed, the arms and the lower body are remained intact. The complex meaning of this statue is yet to be explored. There exist a certain tendency to believe that this statue might have bore the resemblances of wild animals on its upper body. A leopard, wild boar or a lion with arms that are either holding or protecting a human head. This connection is established on the basis of finds at Nevali Cori, where in multiple motifs, animals are being depicted holding human crania. The statue of Gobekli Tepe could be a composition of such symbolic representations.

5.17

## Skull Preference

Another proposition supported by recently discovered human skull fractures from the site is also worth exploring. Osteological studies released in 2017 have corroborated the higher frequency of human cranial fragments recovered from the site, relative to the assemblage of skeletal tissues belonging to

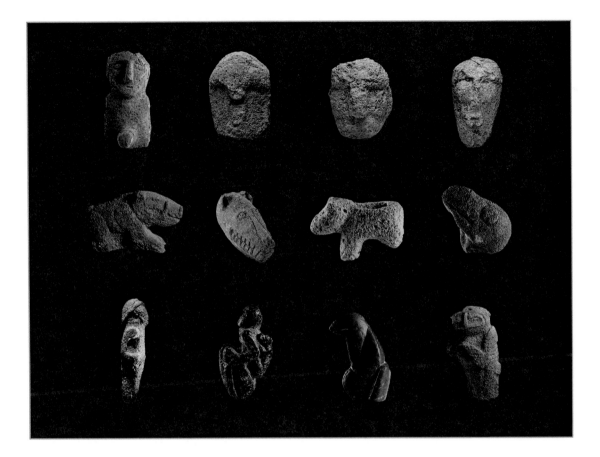

lower body parts. The rate of prevalence is approximately four to one, an indication of high cultural desirability of skull fragments to the people of Gobekli Tepe, that is often loosely described to be connected to a skull cult. Nevertheless, scattered human remains comprise less than one percent of the total skeletal fragments revealed at Gobekli Tepe. It is worth to mention that evidence in support of burial practices has yet to be discovered across the site. There is no indication for the usage of the hill as a burial place.

Analyses of skull fragments have been capable of bringing to the fore the extensiveness of skull treatment traditions at the site. One in every five pieces of identified cranial specimen have yielded posthumous cut marks, application of ochre or evidence

Figure 156. A range of finds unearthed at Gobekli Tepe. The three limestone heads to the top right were all portions of life-size human statues. The top left hand side statue, shows a male lacking arms and lower body. In the middle, the statue of a boar and a leopard head are seen accompanied by a wild boar figurine and a statue of a bird's head with prominent beak and eyes (mid row right). The bottom row from left shows a human statue carved in a conic form. For its shape it is assumed that it was placed inside a pedestal. Second from the left is statue of a man carrying panther on its back. A well preserved and polished figurine of a bird's head is also carved out of a unique red limestone with a hooked beak. The statue of a wild boar is seen at the lower right hand side.

Figure 157. Fragments of frontal and laternal skull bones with posthumous cut marks and perforations unearthed at Gobekli Tepe. Incisions indicate that curation and management of the deceased crania for cultural purposes and modification were common practices at Gobekli Tepe.

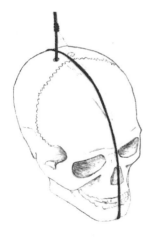

Figure 158. Drilled perforation at the top of the cranium was used to suspend the skull with a cord (red). A hypothetical theory suggests that carvings were used for stabilization purposes, preventing the cord from slipping and keeping the crania in place for cultural purposes.

of ritualistic perforations. These skull fragments are found near enclosures A and D to the Southwestern Depression of the mound and across trenches laid at the Northwestern Depression. It is suggested that skulls might have been hung from the interior wall of pillars of the Gobekli complex, either with respect to the ancestral veneration or based on a loosely theoretical claim that suggests their usage for condemnation of the enemies - no corroborative evidence across the entire region of the Near East has been found to support this hypothesis.

5.19

The enclosures at Gobekli Tepe are devoid of human burials. Although the backfill material, generally contains traces of human remains, it appears that the tradition of internment was not yet practiced by the hunter-gatherers of the time or if so, burials must have taken place out of the boundaries of sanctuaries. Some archaeologists have advocated for the possibility of burials inside stone benches of enclosures and furthermore behind the walls or beneath the central pillars. Excavators up to this point, have avoided destructive and intrusive measures in unearthing all that lies beneath the temples. The recovery of such burials, if they exist, requires undertaking invasive methods, disrupting the stratigraphy of the site, its structural integrity and destroying depositional components within. In other words, these could mount to the partial destruction of Gobekli Tepe that is a universal heritage site.

5.20

## The Cultic Community of Gobekli Tepe

As Klaus Schmidt once explained, what we know of Gobekli Tepe and its people is only the tip of the iceberg. Although, the first sanctuaries erected at the site were examples of the oldest known human structure across the globe, nevertheless, in the time span of two thousand years, the culture and practices of Gobekli Tepe had spread out across the entire landscape of the Near East. It is disputable whether it all started from this

junction of the southern Anatolia, but by the turn of the 9th millennium BCE, the cultic practices, most apparent and extensively documented at Gobekli Tepe had spread out throughout a network of towns, settlements, and sanctuaries in southern Turkey, northern Syria, western Iran and the Levant. Nevali Cori, Cayonu, Catalhouyk, Jerf el Ahmar, Moreybet, Gurcu Tepe, and Hallan Cemi are only a short list of sites associated with this thriving culture, with shared communal buildings and indications of ancestral veneration. Schmidt held the revolutionary belief that for several weeks or months a year, the people of the region would travel to the temple or contemporaneous temples of Gobekli Tepe, taking part in ceremonial rites and contributing to the work of quarrying stone pillars and decorating enclosures. We may never fully get a grasp of what was the purpose for the construction of these monuments, but we know beyond the shadow of doubt, that for

5.21

Figure 159. Catalhoyuk in central Turkey was perhaps the most populated Neolithic settlement in the world. The community hosted well over 5,000 people about 9,000 years ago and it played a crucial role in full transition to the adoption of a Neolithic way of life, farming and animal husbandry. Gobekli Tepe preceded the rise of settlements such as Catalhoyuk by at least a thousand years, but nevertheless it is believed that communal practices and collective undertakings originated at Gobekli Tepe, possibly the first of its kind in history, provided an impetus and a hope for success in similar social endeavours that swept the Near Eastern landscape in the following millennia.

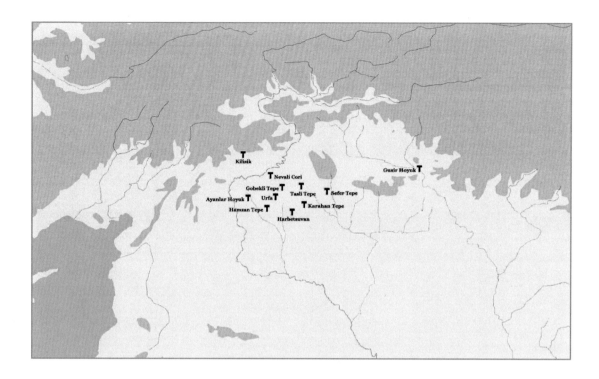

Figure 160. Map of distribution for Pre-pottery Neolithic sites of the Near East with communal sanctuaries decorated by T-shaped pillars, similar to those of Gobekli Tepe. To this date, eleven regional site with round-shaped or rectangular enclosures supported by limetone T-shaped pillars have been discovered, all centred in the core region of the Golden Triangle.

the people involved, this was the largest collective undertaking they had ever witnessed in their lives. The experience of which might have never fled their living memories. It is safe to suggest that Gobekli Tepe played a central role in the spiritual life of the Neolithic people, emerging out of the ashes of the abandoned temples. The construction of these enclosures and the social expertise required for achieving that might have effectuated the completion of a package of human traits which were prerequisites to the Neolithic Revolution, one of the most significant transitions in human history. Gobekli Tepe, stood right at the centre of this dramatic change.

# 6

## CHAPTER SIX

### BIBLIOGRAPHY, NOTES
### AND REFERENCES

# Books and Dissertations:

Albarella, Umberto; Rizzetto, Mauro; Russ, Hannah et al. 2017 *The emergence of livestock husbandry in Early Neolithic Anatolia* in The Oxford Handbook of Zooarchaeology, Chapter 18, Oxford University Press

Antonello, Pierpaolo; Gifford, Paul 2015 *How we became human : mimetic theory and the science of evolutionary origins*, East Lansing: Michigan State University Press

Arbuckle, Benjamin; Meadow, Richard 2006 *The evolution of sheep and goat pastoralism and social complexity in Central Anatolia*, ProQuest Dissertations Publishing

Aslan, Reza 2017 *God: A Human History,* Random House Publishing Group

Atici, Ahmet 2007 *Before the revolution: A comprehensive zooarchaeological approach to terminal Pleistocene forager adaptations in the western Taurus Mountains, Turkey,* ProQuest Dissertations Publishing

Bachenheimer, Avi Jacob 2015 *Gobekli Tepe; An Introduction to the World's Oldest Temple*, Blurb, Incorporated

Barket, Theresa; Wilke, Philip J. (advisor); Fedick, Scott (committee member) ; Lee, Sang-Hee (committee member); Quintero, Leslie (committee member); Rollefson, Gary (committee member) 2016 *The Tool Kit of Daily Life: Flaked-Stone Production at the Household Level at the Neolithic Site of `Ain Ghazal, Jordan* ProQuest Dissertations Publishing; ProQuest Dissertations and Theses

Bar-Yosef, Ofer.; Valla, François Raymond. Ann Arbor, Mich. 1991 *The Natufian culture in the Levant*: International Monographs in Prehistory

Başgelen, Nezih; Özdoğan, Mehmet 1999 *Neolithic in Turkey: the cradle of civilization: new discoveries*, Volume 1, Arkeoloji ve Sanat Yayınları

Bennallack, Kathleen; Levy, Thomas E. (advisor) ; Algaze, Guillermo (committee member) ; Schoeninger, Margaret (committee member) 2012 *Production of Ritual Material Culture in the Pre-Pottery Neolithic Period in Jordan: Some Methods for Analytical Investigation* ProQuest Dissertations Publishing; ProQuest Dissertations and Theses

Brodsky, Judith K.; Olin, Ferris.; Mason 2012 *The fertile crescent: gender, art, and society* School of the Arts (Rutgers University). Galleries. New Brunswick, N.J. New York, N.Y. : Rutgers University Institute for Women and Art ; Distributed by D.A.P./Distributed Art Publishers

Bystedt, Karen Hardy.; Kubiak-Martens, Lucy. 2016 *Wild Harvest : Plants in the Hominin and Pre-Agrarian Human Worlds.* Havertown : Oxbow Books

Campana, Douglas V. 1989 *Natufian and protoneolithic bone tools : the manufacture and use of bone implements in the Zagros and the Levant* Oxford, England : B.A.R

Carleton, William, 2008 *The end of the Pre-Pottery Neolithic in southwest Asia from the perspective of Catalhoyuk,* ProQuest Dissertations Publishing

Cauvin, Ducos, Pierre 1978 *Tell-Mureybet. 1, Les Niveaux I-XVII, fouilles Van Loon et la phase IV, fouilles.* Auteur Du Texte Éditions du C.N.R.S. (Paris)

Chacon, Richard; Mendoza, Rubén 2017 *Feast, Famine or Fighting? Multiple Pathways to Social Complexity.* Cham: Springer International Publishing

Coinman, Nancy; Clark, Geof (advisor) 1990 *Refiguring the Levantine Upper Paleolithic: A comparative examination of lithic assemblages from the southern Levant* ProQuest Dissertations Publishing; ProQuest Dissertations and Theses

Collins, Andrew 2014 *Gobekli Tepe: Genesis of the Gods: The Temple of the Watchers,* Simon and Schuster

Davies, William.; Charles, Ruth. Havertown 2017 *Dorothy Garrod and the Progress of the Palaeolithic.* Oxbow Books

Demand, Nancy H. 2011 *The Neolithic Revolution/Transition Oxford,* UK: Wiley-Blackwell;The Mediterranean Context of Early Greek History, Chapter 2

Eissenstat, Cigdem; Carter, Elizabeth 2004 *Ritualization of settlement: Conditioning factors of spatial congruity and temporal continuity during the Late Neolithic of southeastern Anatolia,* ProQuest Dissertations Publishing

Finlayson, Bill.; Mithen, Steven J. Havertown 2014 *The Early Prehistory of Wadi Faynan, Southern Jordan: Archaeological Survey of Wadis Faynan, Ghuwayr and Al Bustan and Evaluation of the Pre-Pottery Neolithic A Site of WF16.* : Oxbow Books

Fitzhugh, Ben.; Habu, Junko 2002 *Beyond foraging and collecting: evolutionary change in hunter-gatherer settlement systems,* New York: Kluwer Academic/Plenum Publishers

Gates, Charles 2011 *Ancient Cities The Archaeology of Urban Life in the Ancient Near East and Egypt, Greece and Rome,* 2nd ed.; Florence, Taylor and Francis

Goodarzi-Tabrizi, Shoki; Stronach, David B. 1999 *The worked bone remains of Hallan Cemi Tepesi, an early Neolithic site in southeastern Turkey* ProQuest Dissertations Publishing; ProQuest Dissertations and Theses

Hodder, Ian 2005 *Changing materialities at Çatalhöyük: reports from the 1995-99 seasons;* McDonald Institute for Archaeological Research. London : Cambridge, U.K. British Institute at Ankara; McDonald Institute for Archaeological Research

Hodder, Ian 2006 *Çatalhöyük: the leopard's tale: revealing the mysteries of Turkey's ancient 'town'.* London: Thames & Hudson

Insoll, Timothy ; Croucher, Karina 2011 *Anatolia in The Oxford Handbook of the Archaeology of Ritual and Religion,* Chapter 52, Oxford University Press; 2011

Insoll, Timothy; Verhoeven, Marc 2011 *Retrieving the Supernatural;* Oxford University Press; The Oxford Handbook of the Archaeology of Ritual and Religion, Chapter 50

Jones, Sally-Ann 2000 *Gobekli Tepe: Re-interpreting Ritual and Religion in Pre-pottery Neolithic Anatoloia,* University of Manchester

Kelly, Lynne 2015 *Knowledge and Power in Prehistoric Societies: Orality, Memory, and the Transmission of Culture,* Cambridge University Press

Killebrew, Ann E. ; Steiner, Margreet ; Betts, Alison; Killebrew, Ann E. ; Steiner, Margreet ; Betts, Alison 2013 *The Southern Levant (Transjordan) During the Neolithic Period 1;* Oxford University Press; The Oxford Handbook of the Archaeology of the Levant, c. 8000-332 BCE, Chapter 012

Kuijt, Ian 1995 *New perspectives on old territories: Ritual practices and the emergence of social complexity in the Levantine Neolithic* ProQuest Dissertations Publishing; ProQuest Dissertations and Theses

Kusatman, Berrin 1992 *The origin of pig domestication: With particular reference to the Near East* ProQuest Dissertations Publishing; PQDT - Global

Landis, Don 2015 *Secrets of Ancient Man : Revelations from the Ruins. Green Forest,* New Leaf Publishing Group, Inc.

Laneri, Nicola 2015 *Defining the Sacred: Approaches to the Archaeology of Religion in the Near East,* Havertown: Oxbow Books

Luckert, Karl W. 2013 *Stone Age Religion at Goebekli Tepe,* Triplehood

Makarewicz, Cheryl; Tuross, Noreen 2007 *Evolution of foddering practices in the southern Levantine Pre - Pottery Neolithic,* ProQuest Dissertations Publishing

Mayer, Daniella Bar-Yosef.; Bonsall, Clive.; Choyke, Alice M. Havertown 2017 *Not Just for Show: The Archaeology of Beads, Beadwork, and Personal Ornaments.* Oxbow Books, Limited

Mcmahon, Gregory; Steadman, Sharon; Schmidt, Klaus 2001 *Göbekli Tepe: A Neolithic Site in Southeastern Anatolia,* in The Oxford Handbook of Ancient Anatolia, (10,000-323 BCE), Chapter 42, Oxford University Press

Meiggs, David; Price, T. Douglas 2009 *Investigation of neolithic ovicaprine herding practices by multiple isotope analysis: A case study at PPNB Grittile, southeastern Turkey,* ProQuest Dissertations Publishing

Peasnall, Brian; Zettler, Richard (advisor) 2000 *The round house horizon along the Taurus-Zagros arc: A synthesis of recent excavations of late Epipaleolithic and early aceramic sites in southeastern Anatolia and northern Iraq* ProQuest Dissertations Publishing; ProQuest Dissertations and Theses

Plegge, Joe 2012 *Turkish Stonehenge,* Enterprises

Potts, D. T. 2012 *A Companion to the Archaeology of the Ancient Near East*, Somerset: Wiley

Pyszczynski, Tom; Kesebir, Pelin 2012 *Culture, ideology, morality, and religion: Death changes everything*, American Psychological Association

Rambeau, Claire ; Finlayson, Bill ; Smith, Sam ; Black, Stuart ; Inglis, Robyn Helen ; Robinson, Stuart; Mithen, Steven ; Black, Emily 2011 *Palaeoenvironmental reconstruction at Beidha, Southern Jordan (ca. 18,000-8,500 BP): Implications for human occupation during the Natufian and Pre-Pottery Neolithic* Cambridge University Press

Savard, Manon, *Epipalaeolithic to early neolithic subsistence strategies in the northern fertile crescent: the archaeobotanical remains from hallan çemi, demirköy, m'lefaat and qermez dere* ProQuest Dissertations Publishing; 2005

Scanes, C. G.; Toukhsati, Samia. Saint Louis 2017 *Animals and Human Society.* Elsevier Science & Technology

Schmidt, Klaus 2012 *Göbekli Tepe: A Stone Age Sanctuary in South-Eastern Anatolia*, Ex Oriente

Scranton, Laird 2015 *Point of Origin: Gobekli Tepe and the Spiritual Matrix for the World's Cosmologies*, Simon and Schuster

Ulrich, Carolin; Nordon, Alex 2011, *Gobekli Tepe, der alteste Monumentalbau der Menschheit: Religionswissenschaftliche Uberlegungen zu seiner Nutzung als sakrale Kultstatte oder profaner Allzweckbau*, GRIN Verlag

Vafi, Pamela; Feuer, Bryan 2005 *Çatal Hüyük: A prelude to civilization*, ProQuest Dissertations Publishing

Wasse, Alexander 2000 *The development of goat and sheep herding during the Levantine Neolithic* ProQuest Dissertations Publishing; PQDT - Global

Watts, Christopher 2013 *Relational archaeologies: humans, animals, things*, London ; New York : Routledge

Whitehouse, Harvey; Martin, Luther H 2004 *Theorizing Religions Past: Archaeology*, History, and Cognition, Rowman Altamira

Wright, Katherine; Hole, Frank (advisor) 1992 *Ground stone assemblage variations and subsistence strategies in the Levant, 22,000 to 5,500 b.p. (*Volumes I and II) ProQuest Dissertations Publishing; ProQuest Dissertations and Theses

Yesilyurt, Metin 2014 *Die wissenschaftliche Interpretation von Göbeklitepe: Die Theorie und das Forschungsprogramm*, LIT Verlag Münster

# Journals and Articles

Abbès, F.; Bellot-Gurlet, Provenance of the Jerf el Ahmar (Middle Euphrates Valley, Syria) obsidians *Journal of Non-Crystalline Solids,* 2003, Vol.323(1), pp.162-166

Arnaud, Bernadette, First farmers; a unique Syrian site, flooded after completion of a dam, yielded evidence of one of the world's oldest settlements *Archaeology,* Nov-Dec, 2000, Vol.53(6), p.56(4)

Atakuman, Çiğdem, Architectural Discourse and Social Transformation During the Early Neolithic of Southeast Anatolia *Journal of World Prehistory,* 2014, Vol.27(1), pp.1-42

Bahattin Çelik Karahan Tepe: a new cultural centre in the Urfa Area in Turkey *Documenta Praehistorica,* 01 December 2011, Vol.38, pp.241-254

Bahattin Celik, New Neolithic cult centres and domestic settlements in the light of Urfa Region Surveys *Documenta Praehistorica,* 01 December 2015, Vol.42

Bahattin Celik, A new Pre-Pottery Neolithic site in Southeastern Turkey: Ayanlar Höyük (Gre Hut) *Documenta Praehistorica,* 01 January 2018, Vol.44, pp.360-367

Banning, E; Akkermans, Peter et. al So Fair a House: Göbekli Tepe and the Identification of Temples in the Pre-Pottery Neolithic of the Near East *Current Anthropology,* Oct 2011, Vol.52(5), p.619

Bar-Yosef, Ofer, Climatic Fluctuations and Early Farming in West and East Asia *Current Anthropology,* 01, 24 October August 2011 2011, Vol.52(S4), pp.S175-S193

Busacca, Gesualdo, Places of Encounter: Relational Ontologies, Animal Depiction and Ritual Performance at Göbekli Tepe *Cambridge Archaeological Journal,* 2017, Vol.27(2), pp.313-330

Dietrich, Oliver; Heun, Manfred et. al The role of cult and feasting in the emergence of Neolithic communities. New evidence from Göbekli Tepe, south-eastern Turkey *Antiquity,* Sep 2012, Vol.86(333), pp. 674-695

Dietrich, Oliver; Notroff, Jens et. al Masks and masquerade in the Early Neolithic: a view from Upper Mesopotamia ; Dietrich, Laura Routledge *Time and Mind,* 02 January 2018, Vol.11(1), p.3-21

Fagan, Anna, Hungry architecture: spaces of consumption and predation at Göbekli Tepe Routledge *World Archaeology,* 27 May 2017, Vol.49(3), p.318-337

Finlayson, Bill; Mithen, Steven, Architecture, sedentism, and social complexity at Pre-Pottery Neolithic A WF16, Southern Jordan *Proceedings of the National Academy of Sciences of the United States of America,* May 17, 2011, Vol.108(20), p.8183

Finlayson, Bill, Le village de Jerf el Ahmar (Syrie, 9500-8700 av. J.-C.). L'architecture, miroir d'une société néolithique complexe Cambridge University Press; Dec 2016 *Antiquity,* Vol.90(354), pp.1701-1702

Galili, Ehud; Gopher, Avi et. al Burial Practices at the Submerged Pre-Pottery Neolithic C Site of Atlit-Yam, Northern Coast of Israel *Bulletin of the American Schools of Oriental Research*, 1 August 2005, Issue 339, pp.1-19

Garcea, Elena A.A.; Karul, Necmi, Southwest Asian domestic animals and plants in Africa: Routes, timing and cultural implications *Quaternary International,* 15 August 2016, Vol.412, pp.1-10

Gresky, Julia ; Haelm, Juliane et al. Modified human crania from Göbekli Tepe provide evidence for a new form of Neolithic skull cult *Science Advances*, 2017, Vol.3(6)

Grosman, Leore; Munro, Natalie D. et. al Nahal Ein Gev II, a Late Natufian Community at the Sea of Galilee 2016. "Nahal Ein Gev II, a Late Natufian Community at the Sea of Galilee." *PLoS ONE* 11 (1): e0146647. doi:10.1371/journal.pone.0146647. http://dx.doi.org/10.1371/journal.pone.0146647.

Grosman, Leore; Shaham, Dana et. al A human face carved on a pebble from the Late Natufian site of Nahal Ein Gev II *Antiquity*, Aug 2017, Vol.91(358), pp.1-5

Güler, Gül; Çelik, Bahattin, New Pre-Pottery Neolithic sites and cult centres in the Urfa Region *Documenta Praehistorica*, 2013, Vol.40, pp.291-304

Haldorsen, Sylvi; Akan, Hasan et. al The climate of the Younger Dryas as a boundary for Einkorn domestication *Vegetation History and Archaeobotany,* 2011, Vol.20(4), pp.305-318

Hatice Bilgic; Erdogan E Hakki et al. Ancient DNA from 8400 Year-Old Çatalhöyük Wheat: Implications for the Origin of Neolithic Agriculture *PLoS ONE*, Vol.11(3), p.e0151974

Heun, Manfred; Haldorsen, Sylvi, Reassessing domestication events in the Near East: Einkorn and Triticum urartu *Genome*, June, 2008, Vol.51(6), p.444(9)

Hodder, Ian; Meskell, Lynn, Symbolism, Feasting, and Power at Çatalhöyük A Response to Sutliff and to Hayden *Current Anthropology*, 2012, Vol.53(1), pp.128-129

Kartal, Metin; Kartal, Gizem et. al Chipped stone assemblages of Körtik Tepe (Turkey) *Journal of Archaeological Science:* Reports, June 2018, Vol.19, pp.92-99

Kornienko, Tatiana V. Notes on the Cult Buildings of Northern Mesopotamia in the Aceramic Neolithic Period *Journal of Near Eastern Studies*, April 2009, Vol.68(2), pp.81-102

Kozlowski, Stefan; Kempisty, Andrzej, Architecture of the pre-pottery neolithic settlement in Nemrik, Iraq *World Archaeology*, Feb 1, 1990, Vol.21(3), p.348

Lang, Caroline; Peters, Joris et. al Gazelle behaviour and human presence at early Neolithic Göbekli Tepe, south-east Anatolia Routledge *World Archaeology,* 01 August 2013, Vol.45(3), p.410-429

Le Mort, Françoise; Erim-Özdoğan, Ash, Feu et archéoanthropologie au Proche-Orient (épipaléolithique et néolithique). Le lien avec les pratiques funéraires. Données nouvelles de Çayönü (Turquie) *Paléorient*, 1 January 2000, Vol.26(2), pp.37-50

Lev-Yadun, Simcha; Gopher, Avi, The cradle of agriculture *Science*, Jun 2, 2000, Vol.288(5471), pp.1602-3

Magli, Giulio, Sirius and the project of the megalithic enclosures at Gobekli Tepe *Nexus Network Journal*, July 2016, Vol.18(2), pp.337-346

Mann, Charles C., The birth of religion: we used to think agriculture gave rise to cities and later to writing, art, and religion. Now the world's oldest temple suggests the urge to worship sparked civilization.(Gobekli Tepe) *National Geographic*, June, 2011, Vol.219(6), p.34(26)

McBride, Alexis, Performance and Participation: Multi-Sensual Analysis of Near Eastern Pre-Pottery Neolithic Non-Domestic Architecture *Paléorient*, 1 January 2013, Vol.39(2), pp.47-67

McBride, Alexis, The acoustics of archaeological architecture in the Near Eastern Neolithic Routledge *World Archaeology*, 07 May 2014, p.1-13

Mithen, Steven J. ; Finlayson, Bill et al. An 11 600 year-old communal structure from the Neolithic of southern Jordan *Antiquity*, June 2011, Vol.85, pp.350-364

Okladnikova, Elena A. Fantastic Predator of Kalbak – Tash (High Altai Mountains): Göbekli Tepe Parallels *Procedia - Social and Behavioral Sciences*, 19 March 2014, Vol.120, pp.133-141

Peltenburg, Edgar; Colledge, Sue, Neolithic Dispersals from the Levantine Corridor: a Mediterranean Perspective Routledge *Levant*, 01 January 2001, Vol.33(1), p.35-64

Pöllath, Nadja; Dietrich, Oliver; et. al Almost a chest hit: An aurochs humerus with hunting lesion from Göbekli Tepe, south-eastern Turkey, and its implications *Quaternary International*

Preece, Catherine; Livarda, Alexandra et. al Were Fertile Crescent crop progenitors higher yielding than other wild species that were never domesticated? *New Phytologist*, August 2015, Vol.207(3), pp.905-913

Preece, Catherine; Livarda, Alexandra; Christin et. al, How did the domestication of Fertile Crescent grain crops increase their yields? *Functional Ecology*, February 2017, Vol.31(2), pp.387-397

Pustovoytov, Konstantin; Schmidt, Klaus, Evidence for Holocene environmental changes in the northern Fertile Crescent provided by pedogenic carbonate coatings *Quaternary Research*, 2007, Vol.67(3), pp.315-327

Richter, Tobias  Arranz-Otaegui et.al Shubayqa 6: a new Late Natufian and Pre-Pottery Neolithic A settlement in north-east Jordan *Antiquity*, Dec 2016, Vol.90(354), p.1A,2A,3A,4A,5A

Rowan, Yorke, Gods and scholars: archaeologies of religion in the Near East Cambridge University Press; Oct 2016 *Antiquity*, Vol.90(353), pp.1387-1389

Russell, Nerissa Spirit Birds at Neolithic Çatalhöyük Routledge *Environmental Archaeology*, 10 January 2018, p.1-10

Savard, Manon; Nesbitt, Mark, Archaeobotanical evidence for early Neolithic diet and subsistence at M'lefaat (Iraq) *Paléorient*, 1 January 2003, Vol.29(1), pp.93-106

Scham, Sandra, The world's first temple: Turkey's 12,000-year-old stone circles were the spiritual center of a nomadic people. (Turkey's Gobekli Tepe) *Archaeology*, Nov-Dec, 2008, Vol.61(6), p.22-27

Schmidt, Klaus, Göbekli Tepe: Stone Age Sanctuaries in Upper Mesopotamia; Göbekli Tepe: santuarios de la Edad de Piedra en la Alta Mesopotamia *Boletín de Arqueología* PUCP; Núm. 11 (2007): Procesos y expresiones de poder, identidad y orden tempranos en Sudamérica. Segunda parte; 263-288

Schmidt, Klaus, When Humanity Began to Settle Down *German Research,* May 2008, Vol.30(1), pp.10-13

Schmidt, Klaus Göbekli Tepe – the Stone Age Sanctuaries. New results of ongoing excavations with a special focus on sculptures and high reliefs *Documenta Praehistorica*, 01 December 2010, Vol.37, pp.239-256

Sołtysiak, Arkadiusz; Wiercinska, Alina, Human remains from Nemrik, Iraq. An insight into living conditions and burial customs in a Pre-Pottery Neolithic village *Paléorient*, 2015, Vol.41(2), pp.101-114

Spivey Nigel, Art and Archaeology *Greece and Rome*, 2012, Vol.59(2), pp.275-278

Stordeur, D; Jammous, B, Pierre à rainure à décor animal trouvée dans l'horizon PPNA de Jerf el Ahmar (Syrie) *Paléorient*, Jan 1, 1995, Vol.21(1), p.129

Stordeur, Danielle; Der Aprahamian, Gérard et. al Les bâtiments communautaires de Jerf el Ahmar et Mureybet horizon PPNA (Syrie) *Paléorient*, 1 January 2000, Vol.26(1), pp.29-44

Stordeur, Danielle; Abbès, Frédéric, Du PPNA au PPNB: mise en lumière d'une phase de transition à Jerf el Ahmar (Syrie) *Bulletin de la Société préhistorique française*, 1 July 2002, Vol.99(3), pp.563-595

Syria and the Jezirah Taylor & Francis Group *Journal of The Royal Central Asian Society*, 01 July 1940, Vol. 27(3), p.341-341

Tobolczyk, Marta, The World's Oldest Temples in Göbekli Tepe and Nevali Çori, Turkey in the Light of Studies in Ontogenesis of Architecture *Procedia Engineering,* 2016, Vol.161, pp.1398-1404

Valla, François Raymond, The first settled societies - Natufian (12,500-10,200 BP) *The Archaeology of Society in the Holy Land* (1995) 169-185

Verhoeven, Marc, Ritual and Ideology in the Pre-Pottery Neolithic B of the Levant and Southeast Anatolia *Cambridge Archaeological Journal,* 2002, Vol.12(2), pp.233-258

Verit, Ayhan; Kurkcuoglu, Cihat, Paleoandrologic genital and reproductive depictions in earliest religious architecture: Ninth to tenth millennium bc *Urology*, 2005, Vol.65(1), pp.208-210

Watkins, T; Baird, D; Betts, Qermez Dere and the early aceramic neolithic of N. Iraq *Paléorient*, Jan 1, 1989, Vol.15(1), p.19

Willcox, George; Fornite, Sandra, Impressions of wild cereal chaff in pisé from the 10th millennium uncal B.P. at Jerf et Ahmar and Mureybet: Northern Syria *Vegetation History and Archaeobotany*, 1999, Vol.8(1), pp.21-24

Willcox, George, Charred plant remains from a 10th millennium B.P. kitchen at Jerf el Ahmar (Syria) *Vegetation History and Archaeobotany*, 2002, Vol.11(1), pp.55-60

Willcox, George; Fornite, Sandra et.al Early Holocene cultivation before domestication in northern Syria *Vegetation History and Archaeobotany*, 2008, Vol.17(3), pp.313-325

Willcox, George; Stordeur, Danielle, Large-scale cereal processing before domestication during the tenth millennium cal BC in northern Syria *Antiquity*, Mar 2012, Vol.86(331), pp.99-114

Yartah, Thaér, Tell 'Abr 3, un village du néolithique précéramique (PPNA) sur le Moyen Euphrate. Première approche *Paléorient*, 1 January 2004, Vol.30(2), pp.141-158

# NOTES & FURTHER READINGS

## CHAPTER 1

**1.1** For further discussions around human population dynamics in Europe during the Last Glacial Maximum, see:

Human population dynamics in Europe over the Last Glacial Maximum Miikka Tallavaara, Miska Luoto, Natalia Korhonen, Heikki Järvinen, and Heikki Seppä PNAS July 7, 2015. 112 (27) 8232-8237

Risky business: The impact of climate and climate variability on human population dynamics in Western Europe during the Last Glacial Maximum Burke, Ariane ; Kageyama, Masa ; Latombe, Guillaume ; Fasel, Marc ; Vrac, Mathieu ; Ramstein, Gilles ; James, Patrick M.A. Quaternary Science Reviews, 15 May 2017, Vol.164, pp.217-229

Notice that human population in Europe across the higher latitudes was drastically different to the areas near the Mediterranean Sea.

For further discussions around climatic conditions of Anatolia and the Taurus mountains, see:

Fluvial response to climate change during and after the Last Glacial Maximum in Central Anatolia, Turkey Doğan, Uğur Quaternary International, 2010, Vol.222(1), pp.221-229

Glacier response to the change in atmospheric circulation in the eastern Mediterranean during the Last Glacial Maximum Akçar, Naki ; Yavuz, Vural ; Ivy-Ochs, Susan ; Reber, Regina ; Kubik, Peter W. ; Zahno, Conradin ; Schlüchter, Christian Quaternary Geochronology, February 2014, Vol.19, pp.27-41

Glacier advances in northeastern Turkey before and during the global Last Glacial Maximum Reber, Regina ; Akçar, Naki ; Yesilyurt, Serdar ; Yavuz, Vural ; Tikhomirov, Dmitry ; Kubik, Peter W. ; Schlüchter, Christian Quaternary Science Reviews, 1 October 2014, Vol.101, pp.177-192

For vegetation cover across southern Siberia, see:

Last glacial–interglacial vegetation and environmental dynamics in southern Siberia: Chronology, forcing and feedbacks Bezrukova, Elena V. ; Tarasov, Pavel E. ; Solovieva, Nadia ; Krivonogov, Sergey K. ; Riedel, Frank Palaeogeography, Palaeoclimatology, Palaeoecology, 2010, Vol.296(1), pp.185-198

Stable vegetation and environmental conditions during the Last Glacial Maximum: New results from Lake Kotokel (Lake Baikal region, southern Siberia, Russia) Muller, Stefanie ; Tarasov, Pavel E. ; Hoelzmann, Philipp ; Bezrukova, Elena V. ; Kossler, Annette ; Krivonogov, Sergey K. Quaternary International, Oct 20, 2014, Vol.348, p.14(11)

1.2 For the impact of climatic conditions on Neanderthals, see:

Placing late Neanderthals in a climatic context Tzedakis, P ; Hughen, K ; Cacho, I ; Harvati, K Nature, Sep 13, 2007, Vol.449(7159), pp.206-8

Climatic variability and plant food distribution in Pleistocene Europe: Implications for Neanderthal diet and subsistence Hardy, Bruce L. Quaternary Science Reviews, 2010, Vol.29(5), pp.662-679

For temperatures during tha Last Glacial Maximum, see:

Global patterns of declining temperature variability from the Last Glacial Maximum to the Holocene Kira Rehfeld ; Thomas Münch ; Sze Ling Ho ; Thomas Laepple Nature, 2018

A perspective on model-data surface temperature comparison at the Last Glacial Maximum Annan, J.D. ; Hargreaves, J.C. Quaternary Science Reviews, 1 January 2015, Vol.107, pp.1-10

For the impact of change in climate and its effects on formation of refugia, for both animals and humans, see:

Climate refugia: from the Last Glacial Maximum to the twenty-first century Hampe, Arndt ; Rodríguez-Sánchez, Francisco ; Dobrowski, Solomon ; Hu, Feng Sheng ; Gavin, Daniel G. New Phytologist, January 2013, Vol.197(1), pp.16-18

1.3 There is no indication of a single major migration out of Africa. Archaeological evidence corroborate a series of migrations, often out of Africa - but not always - that peak at around 70,000 years ago, but continue afterwards in new waves of movement. Our reference to the exodus out of Africa refers to a number of migrations that reached a high point at round 70 kya.

The loss in animal diversity through the course of the Last Glacial Maximum does not have an isolated impact on Megafauna alone, it also includes a sharp decline in biodiversity of small mammalian populations. For discussions around both, see:

Small mammal diversity loss in response to late-Pleistocene climatic change Blois, Jessica ; Mcguire, Jenny ; Hadly, Elizabeth Nature, Jun 10, 2010, Vol.465(7299), pp.771-4

Species-specific responses of Late Quaternary megafauna to climate and humans Lorenzen, Eline ; Nogués-Bravo et.al Nature, Nov 17, 2011, Vol.479(7373), pp.359-64

For human population of the planet by the end of the last ice age, see:

Demography and Population Problems By Rajendra K. Sharma, page 71

**1.4** For impacts of insolation on inter-glacial periods, see:

Individual contribution of insolation and CO 2 to the interglacial climates of the past 800,000 years Yin, Qiu ; Berger, André Climate Dynamics, 2012, Vol.38(3), pp.709-724

For discussions around volcanic eruptions see:

Magmatic and phreatomagmatic volcanic activity at Mt. Takahe, West Antarctica, based on tephra layers in the Byrd ice core and field observations at Mt. Takahe Palais, Julie M. ; Kyle, Philip R. ; Mcintosh, William C. ; Seward, Diane Journal of Volcanology and Geothermal Research, 1988, Vol.35(4), pp.295-317

Synchronous volcanic eruptions and abrupt climate change ~17.7 ka plausibly linked by stratospheric ozone depletion McConnell, JR ; Burke, A ; Dunbar, NW ; Köhler, P ; Thomas, JL ; Arienzo, MM ; Chellman, NJ ; Maselli, OJ ; Sigl, M ; Adkins, JF ; Baggenstos, D ; Burkhart, JF ; Brook, EJ ; Buizert, C ; Cole-Dai, J ; Fudge, TJ ; Knorr, G ; Graf, HF ; Grieman, MM ; Iverson, N ; McGwire, KC ; Mulvaney, R ; Paris, G ; Rhodes, RH ; Saltzman, ES ; Severinghaus, JP ; Steffensen, JP ; Taylor, KC ; Winckler, G 2017

The Transantarctic Mountains: Rocks, Ice, Meteorites and Water By Gunter Faure, Teresa M. Mensing, page 621

**1.5** For technological breakthroughs of Homo sapiens of the ice age, see:

Henshilwood, Christopher S.; D'errico, Francesco; Marean, Curtis W.; Milo, Richard G.; Yates, Royden (2001). "An early bone tool industry from the Middle Stone Age at Blombos Cave, South Africa: implications for the origins of modern human behaviour, symbolism and language". *Journal of Human Evolution*. 41 (6): 631–678.

The Emergence of Bone Technologies at the End of the Pleistocene in Southeast Asia: Regional and Evolutionary Implications Rabett, Ryan J ; Piper, Philip J Cambridge Archaeological Journal, 2012, Vol.22(1), pp.37-56

Early Human Migrations: Incipient Stages of Old World Peopling Kozlowski, Janusz Diogenes, 2006, Vol. 53(3), pp.9-22,111,113

**1.6** Particular chronology of extinction for the mentioned is disputable. It appears that the last Homo erectus migh have lived in Ngandong, Indonesia at round 50,000 to 26,000 years ago. Neanderthal remains dating to the apex of the Last Glacial Maximum are ubiquitous, ranging from 26,000 to 24,000 years ago. Homo Floresiensis on the other hand, only survived the LGM to go on extinct near the turn of the 12th millennium BP.

For discussions see:

Finlayson C, Pacheco FG, Rodríguez-Vidal J, et al. (October 2006). "Late survival of Neanderthals at the southernmost extreme of Europe". Nature. 443 (7113): 850–853.

Morwood, M. J.; et al. (27 October 2004). "Archaeology and age of a new hominin from Flores in eastern Indonesia". Nature. 431 (7012): 1087–1091.

**1.7** There is a remarkable continuity in stone tool industries prior, during and after the Last Glacial Maximum. Homo sapiens of Europe and the Near East show particularly evident cases of cultural transitions, where a pecific mode of hafting or knapping lithics appears either first in Europe or in the Near East and it travels across the landscape in the course of the following millennia contrary-wise. This indicates archaeological industries were passed down from a generation to the next and were held a valuable componenet of human toolkit in its struggle against climatic conditions.

**1.8** For discussions around the emergence of human language see:

Mirror Neurons and the Evolution of Brain and Language Stamenov, Maxim I.; Gallese, Vittorio. Amsterdam/Philadelphia : John Benjamins Publishing Company; 2002

An evolutionary context for the emergence of language Tattersall, Ian Language Sciences, Nov, 2014, Vol.46, p.199(8)

Note for one thing, description of a Late Palaeolithic period in our discussion points to a particular timeline unrelated to its European or African counterpart. We tend to use Late Palaeolithic as an alternative to Epipalaeolithic and Upper Palaeolithic.

For Ahmarian culture, see:

Variability in Early Ahmarian lithic technology and its implications for the model of a Levantine origin of the Protoaurignacian. Journal of Human Evolution. 82: 67–87.

Goring-Morris, Nigel; Belfer-Cohen, Anna (4 February 2018). The Middle and Upper Paleolithic Archeology of the Levant and Beyond. Springer, Singapore. pp. 87–104

Isaac, Gilead,. "The Upper Paleolithic period in the Levant". Journal of World Prehistory. 5 (2)

For Emiran culture, see:

Lorraine Copeland; P. Wescombe (1965). Inventory of Stone-Age sites in Lebanon, p. 48 & Figure IV, 4, p. 150. Imprimerie Catholique. Retrieved 21 July 2011.

Bosch, Marjolein D. (April 30, 2015). "New chronology for Ksâr 'Akil (Lebanon) supports Levantine route of modern human dispersal into Europe". Proceedings of the National Academy of Sciences of the United States of America. 112 (25).

For Gravettian radiocarbon dating, see:

Germonpré, Mietje; Sablin, Mikhail; Khlopachev, Gennady Adolfovich; Grigorieva, Galina Vasilievna (2008). "Possible evidence of mammoth hunting during the Epigravettian at Yudinovo, Russian Plain". Journal of Anthropological Archaeology. 27 (4): 475–92.

Noiret, Pierre (2013). "De quoi Gravettien est-il le nom?" [Gravettian is the name of what?]. In Marcel Otte. Les Gravettiens. Civilisations et cultures (in French). Paris: Éditions errance. pp. 28–64.

Jacobi, R.M.; Higham, T.F.G.; Haesaerts, P.; Jadin, I.; Basell, L.S. (2015). "Radiocarbon chronology for the Early Gravettian of northern Europe: New AMS determinations for Maisières-Canal, Belgium". Antiquity. 84 (323): 26–40.

1.9 For discussions around post-glacial vegetation, see:

Late-glacial and Early Postglacial Vegetation and Climate Change in the Northeastern Great Plains: Evidence from Pollen and Plant Macrofossil Studies Catherine Helen Yansa University of Wisconsin--Madison, 2002

Postglacial vegetation history as recorded from the subalpine Lake Ribno (NW Rila Mts), Bulgaria Tonkov, Spassimir ; Bozilova, Elissaveta ; Possnert, Goran Central European Journal of Biology, 2013, Vol.8(1), pp. 64-77

The origin and temporal development of an ancient cultural landscape Fletcher, Michael-Shawn ; Thomas, Ian Journal of Biogeography, November 2010, Vol.37(11), pp.2183-2196

1.10 The Kebaran and the Zarzian cultures, respectively centred around the western and the eastern landscape of the Near East have similarities and distinctions. Unfortunately there had not been a comprehensive study of the cross-comparison of their markers and their social and cultural indicators, to the best of the author's knowledge. Although prospects of such an analysis appears rather enthralling.

For discussions around the Kebaran, see:

The Geometric Kebaran occupation and lithic assemblage of Wadi Mataha, Southern Jordan Macdonald, Danielle A. ; Chazan, Michael ; Janetski, Joel C. Quaternary International, 7 March 2016, Vol.396, pp.105-120

Observations on the Geometric Kebaran : a view from Neve David Kaufman, Daniel; Kaufman, Daniyel Investigations in South Levantine Prehistory (1989) 275-285

Art in the Levantine Epi-Palaeolithic: An Engraved Pebble from a Kebaran Site in the Lower Jordan Valley Hovers, Erella Current Anthropology, Jun 1990, Vol.31(3), p.317

The geometric kebaran microlithic assemblage of Ain Miri, Northern Israel Shimelmitz, Ron ; Barkai, Ran ; Gopher, Avi Paléorient, 1 January 2004, Vol.30(2), pp.127-140

For the Zarzian, see:

The Fauna from the Terminal Pleistocene of Palegawra Cave, A Zarzian Occupation Site in Northeastern Iraq Turnbull, Priscilla F. ; Reed, Charles A. Fieldiana. Anthropology, 11 June 1974, Vol.63(3), pp.81-146

Dorothy Garrod and the Progress of the Palaeolithic. Davies, William.; Charles, Ruth. Havertown : Oxbow Books; 2017

Zarzian Darvill, Timothy 2; Oxford University Press; 2008 The Concise Oxford Dictionary of Archaeology

The earliest Neolithic lithic industries of the Central Zagros: New evidence from East Chia Sabz, Western Iran Nishiaki, Yoshihiro ; Darabi, Hojjat Archaeological Research in Asia

Ohalo II is only one amongst a range of Kebaran sites discovered throughout the Levant, but it has been extensively studied. For discussions around Ohalo and its adjacent sites see:

Wooden objects from Ohalo II (23,000 cal BP), Jordan Valley, Israel Nadel, Dani ; Grinberg, Udi ; Boaretto, Elisabetta ; Werker, Ella Journal of Human Evolution, 2006, Vol.50(6), pp.644-662

Plant-food preparation on two consecutive floors at Upper Paleolithic Ohalo II, Israel Snir, Ainit ; Nadel, Dani ; Weiss, Ehud Journal of Archaeological Science, 2015, Vol.53, p.61(11)

Composite Sickles and Cereal Harvesting Methods at 23,000-Years-Old Ohalo II, Israel Iris Groman-Yaroslavski ; Ehud Weiss ; Dani Nadel PLoS ONE, Vol.11(11), p.e0167151

For dogs and their appearance across cultural remains dating to the Kebaran and the Zarzian periods see the following:

Dayan, Tamar (1994), "Early Domesticated Dogs of the Near East" (Journal of Archaeological Science Volume 21, Issue 5, September 1994, Pages 633–640)

Mellaart, James (1976) "The Neolithic of the Near East" (MacMillan)

**1.11** For evidence of arrow shaft straighteners see:

Design and performance of microlith implemented projectiles during the Middle and the Late Epipaleolithic of the Levant: experimental and archaeological evidence Yaroshevich, Alla ; Kaufman, Daniel ; Nuzhnyy, Dmitri ; Bar-Yosef, Ofer ; Weinstein-Evron, Mina Journal of Archaeological Science, 2010, Vol.37(2), pp. 368-388

Dayan, Tamar (1994), "Early Domesticated Dogs of the Near East" (Journal of Archaeological Science Volume 21, Issue 5, September 1994, Pages 633–640)

M. H. Alimen and M. J. Steve, Historia Universal siglo XXI. Prehistoria. Siglo XXI Editores, 1970 (reviewed and corrected in 1994) (original German edition, 1966, titled Vorgeschichte).

For implications of transition from the Kebaran to the Natufian periods, see the dissertation:

Bar-Yosef, Ofer; Belfer-Cohen, Anna (1989). "The Origins of Sedentism and Farming Communities in the Levant". Journal of World Prehistory. 3 (4): 447–498.

and see the following:

Boyd, Brian (1999). "'Twisting the kaleidoscope': Dorothy Garrod and the 'Natufian Culture'". In Davies, William; Charles, Ruth. Dorothy Garrod and the progress of the Palaeolithic. Oxford: Oxbow. pp. 209–223.

Reconstructing prehistoric hunter-gatherer mobility patterns and the implications for the shift to sedentism: A perspective from the Near East Becker, Mark; Bamforth, Douglas B. (advisor) ProQuest Dissertations Publishing; 1999 ProQuest Dissertations and Theses

**1.12** For discussions around Euro-centricism, see:

Hobson, John (2012). The Eurocentric conception of world politics : western international theory, 1760-2010. New York: Cambridge University Press. p. 185.

Hussein Abdilahi Bulhan, Frantz Fanon and the Psychology of Oppression (1985)

**1.13** For the arrangement of Middle Eastern rivers and their cultural and socio-political implications see:

Between the Great Rivers: Water in the Heart of the Middle East Brooks, Davidb. Taylor & Francis Group International Journal of Water Resources Development, 01 September 1997, Vol.13(3), p.291-310

Rivers of Conflict, Rivers of Peace Lowi, Miriam Journal of International Affairs, Summer 1995, Vol.49(1), p. 123

**1.14** For Hasan Dagi and implications of environmental conditions on domestication of rye see:

On the origin of cultivated rye Sencer, H.A. ; Hawkes, J.G. Biological Journal of the Linnean Society, 1980, Vol.13(4), pp.299-313

**1.15** For obsidian explitation of Late Palaeolithic period at southern Caucasus, see:

New Data on the Exploitation of Obsidian in the Southern Caucasus (Armenia, Georgia) and Eastern Turkey, Part 2: Obsidian Procurement from the Upper Palaeolithic to the Late Bronze Age Chataigner, C ; Gratuze, B Archaeometry, Feb 2014, Vol.56(1), pp.48-69

For implications of obsidian use across the broader landscape of prehistoric Near East, see:

A true gift of mother earth: the use and significance of obsidian at Çatalhöyük Carter, Tristan Anatolian Studies, 1 January 2011, Vol.61, pp.1-19

The obsidian artifacts from Netiv Hagdud : chemical characterization and origin. Yellin, Joseph An Early Neolithic Village in the Jordan Valley I (1997) 193-196

The origin of the obsidian artefacts from Mujahiya : a PPNB site in the Golan Heights. Yellin, Joseph; Gopher, Avi Gofer, Avi ; Goldberg, Tel Aviv 19,1 (1992) 94-99

Diversity in obsidian use in the prehistoric and early historic Middle East Campbell, Stuart ; Healey, Elizabeth Quaternary International, 27 February 2018, Vol.468, pp.141-154

Long distance trinket trade : Early Bronze Age obsidian from the Negev Rosen, Steven A. Journal of Archaeological Science 32,5 (2005) 775-784

**1.16** On the Natufian period and the gradual emergence in cultivation of crops, see:

From foraging to farming in the southern Levant: the development of Epipalaeolithic and Pre-pottery Neolithic plant management strategies Asouti, Eleni ; Fuller, Dorian Vegetation History and Archaeobotany, 2012, Vol.21(2), pp.149-162

Paleopathology and the origin of agriculture in the Levant Eshed, Vered ; Gopher, Avi ; Pinhasi, Ron ; Hershkovitz, Israel American Journal of Physical Anthropology, September 2010, Vol.143(1), pp.121-133

On sedentism, see:

Reassessing the Emergence of Village Life in the Near East Byrd, Brian Journal of Archaeological Research, 2005, Vol.13(3), pp.231-290

For further discussions on the role of Gobekli Tepe and religious beliefs on emergence of agriculture see:

The Birth of the Gods and the Origins of Agriculture (New Studies in Archaeology) by Jacques Cauvin, Cambridge University Press; 1 edition (August 20, 2007)

# CHAPTER 2

**2.1** For a general discussion, see:

Rethinking the human revolution: new behavioural and biological perspectives on the origin and dispersal of modern humans Mellars, Paul. Cambridge, U.K. : McDonald Institute for Archaeological Research; 2007

For an argument with respect to the Asian continent, see:

Human adaptation in the Asian Palaeolithic : hominin dispersal and behaviour during the late Quaternary Rabett, Ryan J., 1970- New York : Cambridge University Press; 2012

**2.2** For distinctive archaeobotanical studies on post-glacial changes in vegetation, see:

Novel insights into post-glacial vegetation change: functional and phylogenetic diversity in pollen records Reitalu, Triin ; Gerhold, Pille ; Poska, Anneli ; Pärtel, Meelis ; Väli, Vivika ; Veski, Siim Journal of Vegetation Science, September 2015, Vol.26(5), pp.911-922

Fore general discussions, see:

The origin and temporal development of an ancient cultural landscape Fletcher, Michael-Shawn ; Thomas, Ian Journal of Biogeography, November 2010, Vol.37(11), pp.2183-2196

For focused discussions around the transition, see the dissertation:

Post-harvest intensification in Late Pleistocene Southwest Asia: Plant food processing as a critical variable in

Epipalaeolithic subsistence and subsistence change Wollstonecroft, Mich ProQuest Dissertations Publishing; 2007 PQDT - Global

Or read Bar-Yosef in the follwoing:

On the Nature of Transitions: the Middle to Upper Palaeolithic and the Neolithic Revolution Bar-yosef, Ofer Cambridge Archaeological Journal, 1998, Vol.8(2), pp.141-163

Nimrods, piscators, pluckers, and planters: The emergence of food production Hayden, Brian Journal of Anthropological Archaeology, 1990, Vol.9(1), pp.31-69

**2.3** Main argument is posited by:

Gebel, H. G. K. (2004). There was no centre: The polycentric evolution of the Near Eastern Neolithic. Neo-Lithics, 1(04), 28–32.

Often the paradigm shift is not evident in literature and discussions around the topic. For some complementary information with regards to the paradigm shift, see Frank Hole:

Agricultural sustainability in the semi-arid Near East Hole, F; Hole, F (correspondence author) Climate of the Past, 2007, Vol.3(2), p.3

The early development of agriculture in the ancient Near East: An ecological and evolutionary study Mccorriston, Joy; Hole, Frank A. (advisor) ProQuest Dissertations Publishing; 1992 ProQuest Dissertations and Theses

A Reassessment of the Neolithic Revolution, Hole, Frank Paléorient, 1 January 1984, Vol.10(2), pp.49-60

Further on the paradigm shift:

The role of cult and feasting in the emergence of Neolithic communities. New evidence from Göbekli Tepe, south-eastern Turkey Dietrich, Oliver ; Heun, Manfred ; Notroff, Jens ; Schmidt, Klaus ; Zarnkow, Martin Antiquity, Sep 2012, Vol.86(333), pp.674-695

The Neolithic in transition — how to complete a paradigm shift Watkins, Trevor Routledge Levant, 01 November 2013, Vol.45(2), p.149-158

For discussions around the first farming communities see:

The Origins of Agriculture in the Near East Zeder, Melinda Current Anthropology, Oct 2011, Vol.52, p.S221

First farmers : the origins of agricultural societies Bellwood, Peter S. Malden, Mass. : Blackwell Pub.; 2005

**2.4** For Golden Triangle, see:

Kozlowski, S.K. & Aurenche, O.. 2005. Territories, boundaries and cultures in the Neolithic Near East (British Archaeological Report International series S-1662). Oxford: Archaeopress.

Further, the case is discussed in the following:

Beyond the Pre-Pottery Neolithic B interaction sphere, Eleni Asouti Published online: 26 April 2007 Springer Science+Business Media, LLC 2007

The case is further mentioned in the following:

Lithic analysis and the transition to the Neolithic in the Upper Tigris Valley: recent excavations at Hasankeyf Hoyuk.(Report) Maeda, Osamu Antiquity, 2018, Vol.92(361), p.56(18)

Bachenheimer, Avi - New Insights Derived from Comparative Analysis of the Faunal Remains of Neolithic Çatalhöyük and PPN Göbekli Tepe

**2.5** Discussions provided on modes of cultural, social and technological transitions are hypothetical and are supported by data at hand. Data on its own is not good or bad, but it comes to play when it functions as an evidence for a theory. We have provided multiple complementary arguments and archaeological finds to support the hypothesis put forward which requires further studies.

**2.6** For discussions on initial domestication of goat, see:

The initial domestication of goats (Capra hircus) in the Zagros mountains 10, 000 years ago Zeder, Melinda ; Hesse, Brian Science, Mar 24, 2000, Vol.287(5461), pp.2254-7

The Slow Birth of Agriculture Pringle, Heather Science, Nov 20, 1998, Vol.282(5393), p.1446(1)

**2.7** On Near Eastern geography, see:

The Geography of the Middle East. Longrigg, Stephen.; Longrigg, Stephen H. 1st ed.; Somerset : Routledge; 2017

Middle East : Geography and Geopolitics. Anderson, Ewan.; Anderson, Greg. 8th ed.; Florence : Routledge; 2013

For its changing features, see:

The Changing geography of Africa and the Middle East Chapman, Graham.; Baker, Kathleen M., 1950-; University of London. School of Oriental and African Studies. Department of Geography. London ; New York : Routledge; 1992

**2.8** For changing dynamics of the Persian Gulf see:

Shoreline reconstructions for the Persian Gulf since the last glacial maximum Lambeck, Kurt Earth and Planetary Science Letters, 1996, Vol.142(1), pp.43-57

Holocene shoreline variations in the Persian Gulf: Example of the Umm al-Qowayn lagoon (UAE) Bernier, Paul ; Dalongeville, Rémi ; Dupuis, Bernard ; de Medwecki, Vincent Quaternary International, 1995, Vol.29, pp.95-103

Overview of multi-level study on coastal processes and shoreline evolution at Northern Persian Gulf and Oman Sea.(Report) Shanehsazzadeh, Ahmad ; Parsa, Reza Ocean and Coastal Management, Nov, 2013, Vol. 84, p.163(11)

For Atlit Yam see the following:

The submerged Pre-Pottery Neolithic water well of Atlit-Yam, northern Israel, and its palaeoenvironmental implications Galili, Ehud ; Nir, Yaacov The Holocene, 1993, Vol.3(3), pp.265-270

Burial practices at the submerged Pre-Pottery Neolithic C site of Atlit-Yam, northern coast of Israel Galili, Ehud, Bulletin of the American Schools of Oriental Research 339 (2005) 1-19

Activities at final Pre-Pottery Neolithic (PPNC) fishing village revealed through microwear analysis of bifacial flint tools from the submerged Atlit-Yam site, Israel Yerkes, Richard W. ; Galili, Ehud ; Barkai, Ran Journal of Archaeological Science, August 2014, Vol.48, pp.120-128

**2.9** For general arguments on change in sea levels and its impacts, see:

Present-day post-glacial sea level change far from the Late Pleistocene ice sheets: Implications for recent analyses of tide gauge records Mitrovica, Jerry X. ; Davis, James L. Geophysical Research Letters, 15 September 1995, Vol.22(18), pp.2529-2532

**2.10** For patterns of change, see:

Seasonally varying footprint of climate change on precipitation in the Middle East Tabari, Hossein ; Willems, Patrick Scientific Reports, 2018, Vol.8(4435), pp.1-10

For soil salinity, see:

Developments in Soil Salinity Assessment and Reclamation: Innovative Thinking and Use of Marginal Soil and Water Resources in Irrigated Agriculture Shabbir A. Shahid, Mahmoud A. Abdelfattah, Faisal K. Taha Springer Science & Business Media, 15 Jan. 2013

Salinity and irrigation agriculture in antiquity Diyala Basin archaeological projects: report on essential results, 1957-58 Thorkild Jacobsen Undena Publications, 1982

For discussions around solar irradiation, see:

Modeling Solar Radiation at the Earth's Surface: Recent Advances Viorel Badescu Springer Science & Business Media, 1 Feb. 2008

**2.11** For discussions on the Near Eastern favourable arc, see:

The emergence of agriculture Smith, Bruce D. (Bruce David), 1946- New York : Scientific American Library : Distributed by W.H. Freeman; 1995

Ancient Agriculture: From Foraging to Farming Michael Woods, Mary Boyle Woods Twenty-First Century

Books, 2000

**2.12** On the Neolithic founder crops, see:

The neolithic soutwest Asian founder crops: their biology and archaeology Weiss, Ehud ; Zohary, Daniel Current Anthropology, Oct, 2011, Vol.52(5), p.S237(18)

"Founder crops" v. wild plants: Assessing the plant-based diet of the last hunter-gatherers in southwest Asia Arranz-Otaegui, Amaia ; González Carretero, Lara ; Roe, Joe ; Richter, Tobias Quaternary Science Reviews, 15 April 2018, Vol.186, pp.263-283

A critical review of the protracted domestication model for Near-Eastern founder crops: linear regression, long-distance gene flow, archaeological, and archaeobotanical evidence Heun, Manfred ; Abbo, Shahal ; Lev - Yadun, Simcha ; Gopher, Avi Journal Of Experimental Botany, 2012, Vol. 63(12), pp.4333-4341

**2.13** For the Natufians harvesting crops, see:

From foraging to farming in the southern Levant: the development of Epipalaeolithic and Pre-pottery Neolithic plant management strategies Asouti, Eleni ; Fuller, Dorian Vegetation History and Archaeobotany, 2012, Vol.21(2), pp.149-162

Paleopathology and the origin of agriculture in the Levant Eshed, Vered ; Gopher, Avi ; Pinhasi, Ron ; Hershkovitz, Israel American Journal of Physical Anthropology, September 2010, Vol.143(1), pp.121-133

For impact of climatic conditions on boundaries of growth for the founder crops, see:

The climate of the Younger Dryas as a boundary for Einkorn domestication Haldorsen, Sylvi ; Akan, Hasan ; Çelik, Bahattin ; Heun, Manfred Vegetation History and Archaeobotany, 2011, Vol.20(4), pp.305-318

**2.14** For the Dump-Heap hypothesis, see the following:

On the Origin of Near Eastern Founder Crops and the 'Dump-heap Hypothesis' Abbo, Shahal ; Gopher, Avi ; Rubin, Baruch ; Lev-Yadun, Simcha Genetic Resources and Crop Evolution, 2005, Vol.52(5), pp. 491-495

Reassessing the Emergence of Village Life in the Near East Byrd, Brian Journal of Archaeological Research, 2005, Vol.13(3), pp.231-290

**2.15** On implications of animal interaction, see:

Gazelle behaviour and human presence at early Neolithic Göbekli Tepe, south-east Anatolia Lang, Caroline ; Peters, Joris ; Pöllath, Nadja ; Schmidt, Klaus ; Grupe, Gisela Routledge World Archaeology, 01 August 2013, Vol.45(3), p.410-429

The Evolutionary Ecology of Animal Migration Robin Baker Holmes & Meier Publishers, 1978

The Origins and Spread of Domestic Animals in Southwest Asia and Europe Sue Colledge, James Conolly,

Keith Dobney, Katie Manning, Stephen Shennan Routledge, 16 Jun. 2016

**2.16** On Jarmo and the Zagros cluster, see:

Prehistoric archeology along the Zagros Flanks Linda S. Braidwood Oriental Institute of the University of Chicago, 1983

Bones and Identity: Zooarchaeological Approaches to Reconstructing Social and Cultural Landscapes in Southwest Asia Nimrod Marom, Reuven Yeshuran, Lior Weissbrod, Guy Bar-Oz Oxbow Books, 31 Jul. 2016

The Domestication and Exploitation of Plants and Animals Peter John Ucko, G. W. Dimbleby Transaction Publishers, 1 Jan. 2007

**2.17** On Ali Kosh, see:

'Seek, and you shall find': a new era at the dawn of domestication and sedentism in Early Neolithic Iran Alizadeh, Abbas Cambridge University Press; Sep 2014 Antiquity, Vol.88(341), pp.977-980

Prehistory and Human Ecology of the Deh Luran Plain: An Early Village Sequence from Khuzistan, Iran Book by Frank Hole, James A. Neely, and Kent V. Flannery, 1969

**2.18** For current discourse on neolithic settlements and the order of domestication, see:

Evolution of Wild Emmer and Wheat Improvement: Population Genetics, Genetic Resources, and Genome Organization of Wheat's Progenitor, Triticum dicoccoides E. Nevo, A.B. Korol, A. Beiles, T. Fahima Springer Science & Business Media, 29 Jun. 2013

Archaeozoology of the Near East Marjan Mashkour, Mark Beech Oxbow Books, 28 Feb. 2017

The cradle of agriculture Lev-Yadun, Simcha ; Gopher, Avi ; Abbo, Shahal Science, Jun 2, 2000, Vol. 288(5471), pp.1602-3

Documenting the initial appearance of domestic cattle in the Eastern Fertile Crescent (northern Iraq and western Iran) Arbuckle, Benjamin S. ; Price, Max D. ; Hongo, Hitomi ; Öksüz, Banu

The early management of cattle (Bos taurus) in Neolithic central Anatolia Arbuckle, Benjamin ; Makarewicz, Cheryl Antiquity, Sep 2009, Vol.83(321), pp.669-686

Herding Strategies at Neolithic Gritille Stein, Gil Expedition, Jan 1, 1986, Vol.28(2), p.35

**2.20** For genetics of domestication, see:

People, plants, and genes the story of crops and humanity Murphy, Denis J. Oxford ; New York : Oxford University Press; 2007

Documenting Domestication: New Genetic and Archaeological Paradigms Melinda A. Zeder, Daniel G.

Bradley, Bruce D. Smith, Eve Emshwiller University of California Press, 20 Jun. 2006

Domestication of Plants in the Old World: The Origin and Spread of Domesticated Plants in Southwest Asia, Europe, and the Mediterranean Basin Daniel Zohary, Maria Hopf, Ehud Weiss OUP Oxford, 2012

**2.21** For the analysis of inbreeding in domestication, see:

Evolution of crop species: genetics of domestication and diversification Rachel S. Meyer ; Michael D. Purugganan Nature Reviews Genetics, 2013, Vol.14(12), p.840

A simulation of the effect of inbreeding on crop domestication genetics with comments on the integration of archaeobotany and genetics: a reply to Honne and Heun Allaby, Robin ; Brown, Terence ; Fuller, Dorian Vegetation History and Archaeobotany, 2010, Vol.19(2), pp.151-158

**2.22** Designations are often tentaive. For regional primacies in case of sheep, see:

Early Animal Domestication and Its Cultural Context Pam J. Crabtree, Douglas V. Campana, Kathleen Ryan UPenn Museum of Archaeology, 1989

Simmons, Paula; Carol Ekarius (2001). Storey's Guide to Raising Sheep. North Adams, MA: Storey Publishing LLC.

Krebs, Robert E.; Carolyn A. (2003). Groundbreaking Scientific Experiments, Inventions & Discoveries of the Ancient World. Westport, CT: Greenwood Press.

Chessa, B.; Pereira, F.; Arnaud,et al. (2009). "Revealing the History of Sheep Domestication Using Retrovirus Integrations". Science. 324 (5926): 532–536.

For cattle, see:

McTavish, E.J.; Decker, J.E.; Schnabel, R.D.; Taylor, J.F.; Hillis, D.M.year=2013 (2013). "New World cattle show ancestry from multiple independent domestication events". Proc. Natl. Acad. Sci. U.S.A. 110 (15): E1398–406.

For pig, see:

Ancient DNA, pig domestication, and the spread of the Neolithic into Europe Larson, Greger ; Albarella, Umberto ; Dobney, Keith ; Rowley-Conwy, Peter Proceedings of the National Academy of Sciences of the United States of America, Sep 25, 2007, Vol.104(39), p.15276

Worldwide phylogeography of wild boar reveals multiple centers of pig domestication Larson, Greger ; Dobney, Keith ; Albarella, Umberto ; Fang, Meiying ; Matisoo-Smith, Elizabeth ; Robins, Judith ; Lowden, Stewart ; Finlayson, Heather ; Brand, Tina ; Willerslev, Eske ; Rowley-Conwy, Peter ; Andersson, Leif ; Cooper, Alan Science (New York, N.Y.), 11 March 2005, Vol.307(5715), pp.1618-21

**2.23** For general discussions, see:

Human Evolutionary Genetics: Origins, Peoples & Disease Mark Jobling, Matthew Hurles, Chris Tyler-Smith Garland Science, 25 Jun. 2013

Deep Ancestry: Inside the Genographic Project Spencer Wells National Geographic Books, 2006

For genetic evidence of a demic diffusion, see:

Genetic evidence for the spread of agriculture in Europe by demic diffusion. (migration of Neolithic farmers from the Near East about 9,000 years ago) Sokal, Robert R. ; Oden, Neal L. ; Wilson, Chester Nature, May 9, 1991, Vol.351(6322), p.143(3)

Origins and genetic legacy of Neolithic farmers and hunter-gatherers in Europe Skoglund, Pontus ; Malmström, Helena ; Raghavan, Maanasa ; Storå, Jan ; Hall, Per ; Willerslev, Eske ; Gilbert, M Thomas P ; Götherström, Anders ; Jakobsson, Mattias Science (New York, N.Y.), 27 April 2012, Vol.336(6080), pp.466-9

Ancient DNA Reveals Key Stages in the Formation of Central European Mitochondrial Genetic Diversity Brandt, Guido ; Haak, Wolfgang ; Adler, Christina et.al Science, Oct 11, 2013, Vol.342(6155), pp.257-261

For frequency in Europe, see:

The Eastern side of the Westernmost Europeans: Insights from subclades within Y-chromosome haplogroup J-M304 Manco, Licínio ; Albuquerque, Joana ; Sousa, Maria Francisca et.al American Journal of Human Biology, March 2018, Vol.30(2)

# CHAPTER 3

**3.1** Records are examined and provided by the author.

For additional contextual information, read Schmidt:

Göbekli Tepe, Southeastern Turkey: A Preliminary Report on the 1995-1999 Excavations Schmidt, Klaus Paléorient, 1 January 2000, Vol.26(1), pp.45-54

**3.2** For theories on PPN origin, see:

Göbekli Tepe – the Stone Age Sanctuaries. New results of ongoing excavations with a special focus on sculptures and high reliefs Klaus Schmidt Documenta Praehistorica, 01 December 2010, Vol.37, pp.239-256

Furthermore, carbondating of samples support the hypothesis that Gobekli Tepe was built during the PPN period. Results come in the following chapters.

**3.3** See Mithens on Gobekli Tepe, general topography and geographical context:

After the Ice: A Global Human History, 20,000-5000 BC Steven Mithen Harvard University Press, 2006

**3.4** For additional contextual information, see:

New light on Neolithic revolution in south-west Asia Watkins, Trevor Antiquity, Sep 2010, Vol.84(325), pp. 621-634

and again see Schmidt:

Göbekli Tepe, Southeastern Turkey: A Preliminary Report on the 1995-1999 Excavations Schmidt, Klaus Paléorient, 1 January 2000, Vol.26(1), pp.45-54

**3.5** Significance of Syrian Jezirah is missing from the current studies. For its importance, see a paper from 1940:

Syria and the Jezirah Taylor & Francis Group Journal of The Royal Central Asian Society, 01 July 1940, Vol. 27(3), p.341-341

Also see Cauvin:

The Birth of the Gods and the Origins of Agriculture Jacques Cauvin Cambridge University Press, 27 Jul. 2000

**3.6** For detailed stratographic analysis, composition and interpretation, see:

Soils and soil sediments at Göbekli Tepe, southeastern Turkey: A preliminary report Pustovoytov, Konstantin; Fuchs, M. ; Deckers, K. Geoarchaeology, October 2006, Vol.21(7), pp.699-719

**3.7** For Breasted and his life see:

American Egyptologist: The Life of James Henry Breasted and the Creation of His Oriental Institute, Abt, Thomason, Allison Karmel Vitae Scholasticae, Spring, 2013, Vol.30(1), p.53(5)

For his works, see:

Ancient Times a History of the Early World: An Introduction to the Study of Ancient History and the Career of Early Man James Henry Breasted Charles River Editors, 22 Mar. 2018

The Dawn of Conscience James Henry Breasted CreateSpace Independent Publishing Platform, 18 Mar. 2018

Survey of the Ancient World 1919 James Henry Breasted Kessinger Publishing, 1 Apr. 2003

**3.8** See discussions by Asouti

Beyond the Pre-Pottery Neolithic B interaction sphere, Eleni Asouti Published online: 26 April 2007 Springer Science+Business Media, LLC 2007

**3.10** For Kenyon:

Dame Kathleen Kenyon: Digging Up the Holy Land Miriam C Davis Routledge, 16 Sep. 2016

Jericho Kenyon, Kathleen M. Archaeology and Old Testament Study (1967) 264-275

Excavations at Jericho 3. The Architecture and Stratigraphy of the Tell Hole, Frank ; Kenyon, Kathleen M. ; Holland, Thomas A. American Journal of Archaeology, 04/1983, Vol.87(2), p.278

For Braidwood and Cambel, see:

Prehistoric Investigations in Southeastern Turkey Braidwood, Robert J. ; Çambel, Halet ; Watson, Patty Jo Science, 13 June 1969, Vol.164(3885), pp.1275-1276

Introduction, Braidwood, Robert, *Expedition*, Jan 1, 1986, Vol.28(2), p.2

Jericho and its Setting in Near Eastern History Braidwood, Robert Antiquity, Jan 1, 1957, Vol.31, p.73

**3.11** For Nevali Cori and Gobekli Tepe, see:

The World's Oldest Temples in Göbekli Tepe and Nevali Çori, Turkey in the Light of Studies in Ontogenesis of Architecture Tobolczyk, Marta Procedia Engineering, 2016, Vol.161, pp.1398-1404

Masks and masquerade in the Early Neolithic: a view from Upper Mesopotamia Dietrich, Oliver ; Notroff, Jens ; Dietrich, Laura Routledge Time and Mind, 02 January 2018, Vol.11(1), p.3-21

The place that caused the Neolithic James, N Cambridge University Press; Sep 2007 Antiquity, Vol.81(313), pp.784-786

**3.12** For complementary information on Nevali Cori, Hauptmann and finds, see:

Pre-Pottery Neolithic Clay Figurines from Nevali Çori, Turkey Maria Thaís Crepaldi Affonso ; Ernest Pernicka Internet Archaeology, 01 October 2000, Issue 9

Stable isotopes and dietary adaptations in humans and animals at pre-pottery Neolithic Nevallı Çori, southeast Anatolia Lösch, Sandra ; Grupe, Gisela ; Peters, Joris American Journal of Physical Anthropology, October 2006, Vol.131(2), pp.181-193

**3.13** On Benedict, see:

Concrete Planet: The Strange and Fascinating Story of the World's Most Common Man-Made Material Robert Courland Prometheus Books, 2011

Life in Neolithic Farming Communities: Social Organization, Identity, and Differentiation Ian Kuijt Springer Science & Business Media, 2006

Discussions with Savak were conducted by the author, 2013.

**3.14** For chronology of excavations, see:

Göbekli Tepe, Southeastern Turkey: A Preliminary Report on the 1995-1999 Excavations Schmidt, Klaus Paléorient, 1 January 2000, Vol.26(1), pp.45-54

Göbekli Tepe: A Neolithic Site in Southeastern Anatolia Schmidt, Klaus Oxford University Press; 2011 The Oxford Handbook of Ancient Anatolia, (10,000-323 BCE)

**3.15** See the following for general information:

So Fair a House: Göbekli Tepe and the Identification of Temples in the Pre-Pottery Neolithic of the Near East/Comments/Reply Banning, E ; Akkermans, Peter ; Baird, Douglas ; Goring-Morris, Nigel ; Belfer-Cohen, Anna ; Hauptmann, Harald ; Hodder, Ian ; Kuijt, Ian ; Meskell, Lynn ; Özdogan, Mehmet ; Rosenberg, Michael ; Verhoeven, Marc Current Anthropology, Oct 2011, Vol.52(5), p.619

The birth of religion: we used to think agriculture gave rise to cities and later to writing, art, and religion. Now the world's oldest temple suggests the urge to worship sparked civilization.(Gobekli Tepe) Mann, Charles C. National Geographic, June, 2011, Vol.219(6), p.34(26)

The world's first temple: Turkey's 12,000-year-old stone circles were the spiritual center of a nomadic people.(Turkey's Gobekli Tepe)(Cover story) Scham, Sandra Archaeology, Nov-Dec, 2008, Vol.61(6), p. 22-27

Sirius and the project of the megalithic enclosures at Gobekli Tepe Magli, Giulio; Magli, Giulio (correspondence author) Nexus Network Journal, July 2016, Vol.18(2), pp.337-346

**3.16** For composition of the site, see:

Soils and soil sediments at Göbekli Tepe, southeastern Turkey: A preliminary report Pustovoytov, Konstantin; Fuchs, M. ; Deckers, K. Geoarchaeology, October 2006, Vol.21(7), pp.699-719

**3.17** In addition, Figure 124 conatins full detailed record of pillars, their features and interpretations.

**3.18** Stratigraphic analyses are based on:

Göbekli Tepe, Southeastern Turkey: A Preliminary Report on the 1995-1999 Excavations Schmidt, Klaus Paléorient, 1 January 2000, Vol.26(1), pp.45-54

Soils and soil sediments at Göbekli Tepe, southeastern Turkey: A preliminary report Pustovoytov, Konstantin; Fuchs, M. ; Deckers, K. Geoarchaeology, October 2006, Vol.21(7), pp.699-719

**3.19** For dating see:

B. Kromer, K. Schmidt, Two Radiocarbon Dates from Göbekli Tepe, South Eastern Turkey, Neo-Lithics 3/98, 1998, 8-9.

O. Dietrich, C. Köksal-Schmidt, J. Notroff, K. Schmidt, Establishing a Radiocarbon Sequence for Göbekli Tepe. State of Research and New Data, Neo-Lithics 1/2013, 36-41.

K. Schmidt, Göbekli Tepe. Southeastern Turkey. A Preliminary Report on the 1995-1999 Excavations, Paléorient 26/2001, 45-54.

O. Dietrich, Radiocarbon dating the first temples of mankind. Comments on 14C-Dates from Göbekli Tepe. Zeitschrift für Orient-Archäologie 4, 2011, 12-25.

K. Pustovoytov, 14C Dating of Pedogenic Carbonate Coatings on Wall Stones at Göbekli Tepe (Southeastern Turkey). Neo-Lithics 2/2002, 3-4.

K. Pustovoytov, H. Taubald, Stable Carbon and Oxygen Isotope Composition of Pedogenic Carbonate at Göbekli Tepe (Southeastern Turkey) and its Potential for Reconstructing Late Quaternary Paleoenviroments in Upper Mesopotamia. Neo-Lithics 2/2003, 25-32.

K. Pustovoytov, K. Schmidt, H. Parzinger, Radiocarbon dating of thin pedogenic carbonate laminae from Holocene archaeological sites. The Holocene 17. 6, 2007, 835-843.

O. Dietrich, K. Schmidt, A radiocarbon date from the wall plaster of enclosure D of Göbekli Tepe, Neo-Lithics 2/2010, 82-83.

# CHAPTER 4

**4.1** That is in essence the analysis of T-shaped pillars in the context of Gobekli Tepe cultural remains and furthermore, in the context of regional architecture. The study of Gobekli Tepe's pillars in the context of the remains doscovered over the hill itself could be divided into sub-categories, such as their stratigraphic significance, their symbolic meaning and their architectural importance.

**4.2** For Jerf el-Ahmar see:

Large-scale cereal processing before domestication during the tenth millennium cal BC in northern Syria Willcox, George ; Stordeur, Danielle Antiquity, Mar 2012, Vol.86(331), pp.99-114

JERF EL AHMAR: UN NOUVEAU SITE DE L'HORIZON PPNA SUR LE MOYEN EUPHRATE SYRIEN Stordeur, Danielle ; Helmer, Daniel ; Willcox, George Bulletin de la Société préhistorique française, 1 April 1997, Vol.94(2), pp.282-285

Les bâtiments communautaires de Jerf el Ahmar et Mureybet horizon PPNA (Syrie) Stordeur, Danielle ; Der Aprahamian, Gérard ; Brenet, Michel ; Roux, J.C. Paléorient, 1 January 2000, Vol.26(1), pp.29-44

Du PPNA au PPNB: mise en lumière d'une phase de transition à Jerf el Ahmar (Syrie) Stordeur, Danielle ; Abbès, Frédéric Bulletin de la Société préhistorique française, 1 July 2002, Vol.99(3), pp.563-595

Pierre à rainure à décor animal trouvée dans l'horizon PPNA de Jerf el Ahmar (Syrie) Stordeur, D ; Jammous,

B Paléorient, Jan 1, 1995, Vol.21(1), p.129

For Cayonu, see:

Beginnings of Village-Farming Communities in Southeastern Turkey: Çayönü Tepesi, 1978 and 1979 Braidwood, Robert J. ; Çambel, Halet ; Schirmer, Wulf Routledge Journal of Field Archaeology, 01 January 1981, Vol.8(3), p.249-258

Some aspects of building at the 'aceramic-neolithic' settlement of Çayönü Tepesi Schirmer, Wulf Taylor & Francis Group World Archaeology, 01 February 1990, Vol.21(3), p.363-387

For Nevali Cori and Hauptmann, see a range of articles all published in Recent Archaeological Research in Turkey, including:

Recent Archaeological Research in Turkey Erim, Kenan T. ; Morganstern, James ; Laviosa, Clelia ; Bilgi, Önder ; Hauptmann, Harald ; Radt, W. ; Le Roy, M. Christian Anatolian Studies, 1 January 1982, Vol.32, pp.9-22

Recent Archaeological Research in Turkey Naumann, R. ; Erim, Kenan ; Gonnet, Hatice ; Cauvin, Jacques ; Aurenche, Olivier ; Vetters, H. ; Erdemgil, Selahattin ; Frei, Peter ; De Vries, Keith ; Roodenberg, J. J. ; Alkım, U. Bahadır ; Bakır, Temris ; Mellink, Machteld ; Marfoe, Leon ; Duru, Refik ; Hauptmann, Harald ; Harrison, R. M. ; Müller-Wiener, Wolfgang ; Radt, W. ; Greenewalt,, Crawford H. ; Le Roy, M. Christian Anatolian Studies, 1 January 1981, Vol.31, pp.177-208

Recent Archaeological Research in Turkey Akok, Mahmut ; Russell, James ; Erim, Kenan ; Sahin, Sencer ; Chauvin, Jacques ; Aurenche, Olivier ; Çambel, Halet ; Korfmann, Manfred ; Morganstern, James ; Vetters, H. ; Büyükkolancı, Mustafa ; Frei, Peter ; De Vries, Keith ; Behm-Blancke, M. R. ; Peschlow, Anneliese ; Doruk, Seyhan ; Laviosa, Clelia ; Çiligiroğlu, Altan ; Mellink, Machteld ; Bilgi, Önder ; Duru, Refik ; Hauptmann, Harald ; Metzger, Henri Anatolian Studies, 1 January 1980, Vol.30, pp.201-228

Recent Archaeological Research in Turkey Koşay, Hâmit Z. ; Akok, Mahmut ; Russell, James ; Erim, Kenan ; Erzen, Afif ; Morgenstern, James ; Naumann, R. ; Vetters, H. ; Temizer, Raci ; Fıratlı, N. ; Verzone, Paolo ; Laviosa, Clelia ; Alkım, U. Bahadır ; Akat, Altan ; Mellink, Machteld ; Öğün, Baki ; Ertem, Hayri ; Borchardt, J. ; Hauptmann, Harald ; Radt, W. ; Fleischer, Robert ; Hanfmann, George ; Esin, Ufuk ; Polacco, Luigi Anatolian Studies, 1 January 1975, Vol.25, pp.15-52

**4.3** For Enclosure E, see the following:

O. Dietrich, J. Notroff, K. Schmidt. 2017. Feasting, social complexity and the emergence of the early Neolithic of Upper Mesopotamia: a view from Göbekli Tepe. In: R. J. Chacon, R. Mendoza (eds.), Feast, Famine or Fighting? Multiple Pathways to Social Complexity. New York: Springer, 91-132

For general discussions, see:

K. Schmidt, Göbekli Tepe. Southeastern Turkey. A Preliminary Report on the 1995-1999 Excavations, Paléorient 26/2001, 45-54.

**4.4** For enclosures' condition see:

The World's First Temple Scham, Sandra Archaeology, Nov/Dec 2008, Vol.61(6), p.22

Göbekli Tepe - the Stone Age Sanctuaries. New results of ongoing excavations with a special focus on sculptures and high reliefs Schmidt, Klaus Documenta Praehistorica, 2010, Vol.37, pp.239-256

**4.5** Author's observations. These incisions are not confined to the pillars of Enclosure C. They also appear at Enclosures B and D. The upper surface of pillars sometimes have cup-marks imposed on them, and sometimes they have either incisions and cuts along the length and often along their width. The most prevalent type observed is the incision mark along the length to the front of a pillars head segment.

**4.6** This is the impression that pillars around the periphery of a sanctuary give. When standing somewhere near the central pillars or right at the centre of an enclosure one would be able to see particular reliefs carved over some of the pillars, each telling particular stories of its sort, providing a panoramic viewpoint of what was meant to be sketched.

**4.7** For pillar 43, see the following:

Klaus Schmidt, Animals and a Headless Man at Göbekli Tepe, Neo-Lithics. A Newsletter of Southwest Asian Lithics Research 2/2006, 38-40.

Klaus Schmidt, Göbekli Tepe. A Stone Age Sanctuary in South-Eastern Anatolia. ex oriente e.V.: Berlin (2012): p. 244.

For Jericho's see:

Tell es-Sultan/Jericho in the Context of the Jordan Valley: Site Management, Conservation and Sustainable Development Lorenzo Nigro Lorenzo Nigro, 2006

**4.8** For a general report of the sites near Urfa, see:

New Pre Pottery Neolithic sites and cult centres in the Urfa Region Gül Güler ; Bahattin Çelik ; Mustafa Güler Documenta Praehistorica, 01 December 2013, Vol.40, pp.291-304

Pilgrimage and Household in the Ancient Near East Joy McCorriston Cambridge University Press, 14 Mar. 2011

Approaching Monumentality in Archaeology James F. Osborne SUNY Press, 24 Oct. 2014

For Harbetsuvan, see:

A small-scale cult centre in Southeast Turkey: Harbetsuvan Tepesi Çelik, Bahattin Documenta Praehistorica, 2016, Vol.43, pp.421-428

For Hamzan Tepe, see:

Hamzan Tepe in the light of new finds Çelik, Bahattin Documenta Praehistorica, 2010, Vol.37, pp.257-268

For Ayanlar Hoyuk, see:

A new Pre-Pottery Neolithic site in Southeastern Turkey: Ayanlar Höyük (Gre Hut) Bahattin Celik Documenta Praehistorica, 01 January 2018, Vol.44, pp.360-367

**4.9** For Jerf el-Ahmar see:

JERF EL AHMAR: UN NOUVEAU SITE DE L'HORIZON PPNA SUR LE MOYEN EUPHRATE SYRIEN Stordeur, Danielle ; Helmer, Daniel ; Willcox, George Bulletin de la Société préhistorique française, 1 April 1997, Vol.94(2), pp.282-285

Les bâtiments communautaires de Jerf el Ahmar et Mureybet horizon PPNA (Syrie) Stordeur, Danielle ; Der Aprahamian, Gérard ; Brenet, Michel ; Roux, J.C. Paléorient, 1 January 2000, Vol.26(1), pp.29-44

Du PPNA au PPNB: mise en lumière d'une phase de transition à Jerf el Ahmar (Syrie) Stordeur, Danielle ; Abbès, Frédéric Bulletin de la Société préhistorique française, 1 July 2002, Vol.99(3), pp.563-595

Pierre à rainure à décor animal trouvée dans l'horizon PPNA de Jerf el Ahmar (Syrie) Stordeur, D ; Jammous, B Paléorient, Jan 1, 1995, Vol.21(1), p.129

**4.10** Author's personal discussions with Schmidt, 2012. The emphasis is Schmidt's. He believed that this particular feature is distinguishably significant, as it underlies the identity of Gobekli Tepe's builders.

**4.11** For discussions around the noted sites, refer to:

Holocene Settlement of the Egyptian Sahara: Volume 1: The Archaeology of Nabta Playa Fred Wendorf, Romuald Schild Springer Science & Business Media, 11 Nov. 2013

Tracking the Neolithic House in Europe: Sedentism, Architecture and Practice Daniela Hofmann, Jessica Smyth Springer Science & Business Media, 9 Dec. 2012

Landscapes of Neolithic Ireland Gabriel Cooney Routledge, 6 Dec. 2012

The Significance of Monuments: On the Shaping of Human Experience in Neolithic and Bronze Age Europe Richard Bradley Routledge, 6 Dec. 2012

Arkaim Jesse Russell, Ronald Cohn Book on Demand, 2012

**4.12 - 4.13 - 4.14 - 4.15 - 4.16 - 4.17 - 4.18**

General references are from:

Göbekli Tepe, Southeastern Turkey: A Preliminary Report on the 1995-1999 Excavations Schmidt, Klaus Paléorient, 1 January 2000, Vol.26(1), pp.45-54

Göbekli Tepe – the Stone Age Sanctuaries. New results of ongoing excavations with a special focus on sculptures and high reliefs Klaus Schmidt Documenta Praehistorica, 01 December 2010, Vol.37, pp.239-256

Further data and analysis provided are author's field observations.

# CHAPTER 5

**5.1** Some portholes have been found in-situ, near the lower base of an enclosing wall or in a vertical position providing a window frame to the enclosure, such as one at Enclosure D.

For further information, read:

Klaus Schmidt, Die steinzeitlichen Heiligtümer am Göbekli Tepe, in: Doğan-Alparslan, Meltem – Metin Alparslan – Hasan Peker – Y. Gürkan Ergin (Hrsg.), Institutum Turcicum Scientiae Antiquitatis – Türk Eskiçağ Bilimleri Enstitüsü. Colloquium Anatolicum – Anadolu Sohbetleeri VII, 2008. 59-85.

Klaus Schmidt, Göbekli Tepe, Southeastern Turkey. A Preliminary Report on the 1995-1999 Excavations, Paléorient 26/1, 2001, 45-54.

Joris Peters, Klaus Schmidt, Animals in the Symbolic World of Pre-pottery Neolithic Göbekli Tepe, Southeastern Turkey: a Preliminary Assessment, Anthropozoologica 39.1,2004, 179-218.

**5.2** See the following:

Jens Notroff, Oliver Dietrich, Klaus Schmidt, Gathering of the Dead? The Early Neolithic sanctuaries of Göbekli Tepe, Southeastern Turkey, in: Colin Renfrew, Michael Boyd and Iain Morley (Hrsg.), Death shall have no Dominion: The Archaeology of Mortality and Immortality – A Worldwide Perspective. Cambridge: Cambridge University Press (2016), 65-81.

Oliver Dietrich, Çiğdem Köksal-Schmidt, Cihat Kürkçüoğlu, Jens Notroff, Klaus Schmidt, Göbekli Tepe. A Stairway to the circle of boars, Actual Archaeology Magazine Spring 2013, 30-31.

Hodder, I. & L. Meskell, 2011. A "Curious and Sometimes a Trifle Macabre Artistry". Current Anthropology 52(2), 235-63.

Huth, C., 2008. Darstellungen halb skelettierter Menschen im Neolithikum und Chalkolithikum der Alten Welt. Archäologisches Korrespondenzblatt 38, 493-504.

Schmidt, K, 2013. Von Knochenmännern und anderen Gerippen: Zur Ikonographie halb- und vollskelettierter Tiere und Menschen in der prähistorischen Kunst, in: Sven Feldmann – Thorsten Uthmeier (Hrsg.), Gedankenschleifen. Gedenkschrift für Wolfgang Weißmüller, Erlanger Studien zur prähistorischen Archäologie 1, 195-201.

**5.3** Detailed measurments by author.

**5.4** See an analysis by Watkins:

Trevor Watkins, Architecture and 'theatres of memory' in the Neolithic of southwest Asia, January 2004

**5.5** and **5.6**

For general architecture, stairs and the terrace wall, see Schmidt:

Klaus Schmidt, Göbekli Tepe, in: Mehmet Özdoğan – Nezih Başgelen – Peter Kuniholm (Hrsg.), The Neolithic in Turkey. New Excavations & New Research. The Euphrates Basin, Archaeology and Art Publications (2011): 50-52.

**5.7** General References are from:

Göbekli Tepe, Southeastern Turkey: A Preliminary Report on the 1995-1999 Excavations Schmidt, Klaus Paléorient, 1 January 2000, Vol.26(1), pp.45-54

Göbekli Tepe – the Stone Age Sanctuaries. New results of ongoing excavations with a special focus on sculptures and high reliefs Klaus Schmidt Documenta Praehistorica, 01 December 2010, Vol.37, pp.239-256

**5.8** For lithics, see:

K. Schmidt, Göbekli Tepe. Southeastern Turkey. A Preliminary Report on the 1995-1999 Excavations, Paléorient 26/2001, 45-54.

**5.9** See the following:

Oliver Dietrich, Jens Notroff, A sanctuary, or so fair a house? In defense of an archaeology of cult at Pre-Pottery Neolithic Göbekli Tepe. In: Nicola Laneri (eds.), Defining the Sacred: Approaches to the Archaeology of Religion in the Near East. Oxford: Oxbow (2015), 75-89.

Oliver Dietrich, Jens Notroff, Klaus Schmidt, Feasting, Social Complexity and the Emergence of the Early Neolithic of Upper Mesopotamia: A View from Göbekli Tepe, in: R. J. Chacon and R. G. Mendoza (eds.), Feast, Famine or Fighting? Multiple Pathways to Social Complexity. Studies in Human Ecology and Adaptation 8, New York: Springer (2017), 91-132.

Jens Notroff, Oliver Dietrich, Klaus Schmidt, Gathering of the Dead? The Early Neolithic sanctuaries of Göbekli Tepe, Southeastern Turkey, in: Colin Renfrew, Michael Boyd and Iain Morley (Hrsg.), Death shall have no Dominion: The Archaeology of Mortality and Immortality – A Worldwide Perspective. Cambridge: Cambridge University Press (2016), 65-81.

**5.10 - 5.11**

Lang, C., Peters, J., Pöllath, N., Schmidt, K., Grupe, G. 2013: Gazelle behavior and human presence at early Neolithic Göbekli Tepe, SE Anatolia. Journal of World Archaeology 45, 3, 410-429.

And, on feasting in archaeological contexts:

Dietler, Michael and Brian Hayden (editors) (2001). Feasts: Archaeological and Ethnographic Perspectives on Food, Politics, and Power. Washington, DC: Smithsonian.

5.12 For comparisons to Gurcu Tepe see:

M. Belle Bohn, Ch Gerber, M. Morsch, Klaus Schmidt:. Neolithische Forschungen in Obermesopotamien. Gürcütepe und Göbekli Tepe , In: Istanbul Releases 48, 1998, 5-78.

Klaus Schmidt: Zuerst kam der Tempel, dann die Stadt. Bericht zu den Grabungen am Gürcütepe und am Göbekli Tepe 1996-1999 , In: Istanbul Releases 50, 2000, 5-40.

Klaus Schmidt: Gürcütepe, in Die ältesten Monumente der Menschheit. Vor 12.000 Jahren in Anatolien [Great National Exhibition in 2007 in Baden Baden-Württemberg Landesmuseum Karlsruhe Palace, 20 January to 17 June 2007], ed. from the Badische Landesmuseum Karlsruhe. Theiss, Stuttgart 2007, ISBN 978-3-8062-2072-8, p 94th

Klaus Schmidt: Sie bauten die ersten Tempel. Das rätselhafte Heiligtum der Steinzeitjäger, die archäologische Entdeckung am Göbekli Tepe. Munich, 3rd, expanded and updated edition of 2007.

5.13 Persona conversations with the author.

5.14 Klaus Schmidt: Zuerst kam der Tempel, dann die Stadt. Bericht zu den Grabungen am Gürcütepe und am Göbekli Tepe 1996-1999 , In: Istanbul Releases 50, 2000, 5-40.

5.15 For limestone heads, see:

Badisches Landesmuseum (ed.), Vor 12.000 Jahren in Anatolien. Die ältesten Monumente der Menschheit, Stuttgart 2007.

Bar Yosef, O. and Alon, D., Nahal Hemar Cave, 'Atiqot 18, 1988, 1-81.

Hauptmann, H., The Urfa Region, in: Özdoğan, M., Başgelen, N., Kunıholm, P. (eds.), The Neolithic in Turkey 2. The Euphrates Basin, Istanbul 2011, 85-138.

Jammous, B. and Stordeur, D., Jerf el-Ahmar: un site Mureybetien du moyen Euphrate Syrien, horizon PPNA – Xe millénaire avant JC, in: del Olmo-Lete, G. and Montero Fenollós, J.-L. (eds.), Archaeology of the Upper Syrian Euphrates, the Tishrin Dam Areas, Barcelona 1999, 57-69.

Schmidt, K., Göbekli Tepe: A Stone Age Sanctuary in south-eastern Anatolia, Berlin 2012.

Stordeur, D. and Abbès, F., Du PPNA au PPNB: mise en lumière d'une phase transition à Jerf el Ahmar (Syrie), Bulletin de la Société Préhistorique Française 99 (3), 2002, 563-595.

5.16 Schmidt, K., The Urfa Project 1996, Neo-Lithics 2, 1996, 2-3.

5.17 For the analysis of the Totem Pole, see:

Köksal-Schmidt, Çiğdem, Klaus Schmidt, The Göbekli Tepe "Totem Pole". A First Discussion of an Autumn 2010 Discovery (PPN, Southeastern Turkey), Neo-Lithics 1/10, 74-76.

**5.18 - 5.19 - 5.20**

For skull analysis and contextual information, see:

Modified human crania from Göbekli Tepe provide evidence for a new form of Neolithic skull cult Gresky, Julia ; Haelm, Juliane ; Clare, Lee Science Advances, 2017, Vol.3(6)

**5.21** Personal conversations with Schmidt. For further information, see the following:

New Pre-Pottery Neolithic sites and cult centres in the Urfa Region Gül Güler ; Bahattin Çelik ; Mustafa Güler Documenta Praehistorica, 01 December 2013, Vol.40, pp.291-304

Made in United States
North Haven, CT
01 March 2023

33385073R00095